Carleton Renaissance Plays in Translation

*General Editors:* Donald Beecher, Massimo Ciavolella

*Editorial Advisors:*
    J. Douglas Campbell (Carleton)
    Peter Clive (Carleton)
    Louise George Clubb (Harvard)
    Bruno Damiani (Catholic University of America)
    Louise Fothergill-Payne (Calgary)
    Peter Fothergill-Payne (Calgary)
    Amilcare A. Iannucci (Toronto)
    Jean-Marie Maguin (Montpellier)
    Domenico Pietropaolo (Toronto)
    Anthony Raspa (Chicoutimi)
    José Ruano de la Haza (Ottawa)
    Pamela Stewart (McGill)

Carleton Renaissance Plays in Translation offers the student, scholar, and general reader a selection of sixteenth-century masterpieces in modern English translation, most of them for the first time. The texts have been chosen for their intrinsic merits and for their importance in the history of the development of the theatre. Each volume contains a critical and interpretive introduction intended to increase the enjoyment and understanding of the text. Reading notes illuminate particular references, allusions, and topical details. The comedies chosen as the first texts have fast-moving plots filled with intrigues. The characters, though cast in the stock patterns of the genre, are witty and amusing portraits reflecting Renaissance social customs and pretensions. Not only are these plays among the most celebrated of their own epoch, but they directly influenced the development of the comic opera and theatre throughout Europe in subsequent centuries.

In print:

Odet de Turnèbe, *Satisfaction All Around (Les Contens)*
Translated with an Introduction and Notes by Donald Beecher

Annibal Caro, *The Scruffy Scoundrels (Gli Straccioni)*
Translated with an Introduction and Notes by Massimo Ciavolella and Donald Beecher

Giovan Maria Cecchi, *The Owl (L'Assiuolo)*
Translated with an Introduction and Notes by Konrad Eisenbichler

Jean de La Taille, *The Rivals (Les Corrivaus)*
Translated with an Introduction and Notes by H.P. Clive

Alessandro Piccolomini, *Alessandro (L'Alessandro)*
Translated with an Introduction and Notes by Rita Belladonna

Gian Lorenzo Bernini, *The Impresario (Untitled)*
Translated with an Introduction and Notes by Donald Beecher and Massimo Ciavolella

Jacques Grévin, *Taken by Surprise (Les Esbahis)*
Translated with an Introduction and Notes by Leanore Lieblein and Russell McGillivray

Lope de Vega, *The Duchess of Amalfi's Steward (El mayordomo de la duquesa de Amalfi)*
Translated with an Introduction and Notes by Cynthia Rodriguez-Badendyck

*Comparative Critical Approaches to Rennaisance Comedy*
Edited by Donald Beecher and Massimo Ciavolella

Pietro Aretino, *The Marescalco (Il Marescalco)*
Translated with an Introduction and Notes by Leonard G. Sbrocchi and J. Douglas Campbell

Lope de Rueda, *The Interludes*
Translated with an Introduction and Notes by Randall W. Listerman

Girolamo Bargagli, *The Female Pilgrim (La Pellegrina)*
Translated with an Introduction and Notes by Bruno Ferraro

Leone de Sommi, *A Comedy of Betrothal (Tsahoth B'dihutha D'kiddushin)*
Translated with an Introduction and Notes by Alfred S. Golding in consultation with Reuben Ahroni

*About the Harrowing of Hell: A Seventeenth-Century Ukrainian Play in Its European Context*
Translated with an Introduction and Notes by Irena R. Makaryk

Antonio Mira de Amescua, *The Devil's Slave*
Translated with an Introduction and Notes by Michael D. McGaha and J. M. Ruano de la Haza

Carleton Renaissance Plays in Translation

Two French Biblical Plays:

Antoine de Montchrestien
# Haman

(Anonymous)
# New Tragedy of the Perfidy of Haman

Translated with an Introduction and Notes by

Perry Gethner

Dovehouse Editions Canada
1990

Canadian Cataloguing in Publication Data

Montchretien, Antoine de, ca. 1575–1621
  Haman / Antoine de Montchrestien. New tragedy
of the perfidy of Haman / Anonymous

(Carleton Renaissance plays in translation; 19)
Translation of: Aman; translation of: Tragédie
  nouvelle de la perfidie d'Aman.
Includes bibliographical references.

ISBN 0-919473-70-9

1. Haman (Biblical figure) in fiction, drama, poetry, etc. I. Gethner,
Perry.
II. Title. III. Title: New tragedy of the perfidy of Haman. IV. Series.

PQ1647.M4A4314 1990     842'.4     C90-090016-4

Copyright © Dovehouse Editions Inc., 1990
For distribution write to:
    Dovehouse Editions Inc.
    32 Glen Avenue
    Ottawa, Canada
    K1S 2Z7

For information on the series write to:
    Carleton Renaissance Plays in Translation
    Department of English
    Carleton University
    Ottawa, Canada
    K1S 5B6

No part of this book may be translated or reproduced in any form,
by print, photoprint, microfilm, or any other means, without written
permission from the publisher.

Typeset by Humanities Publishing Services, University of Toronto.

Printed in Canada by Imprimerie Gagné Ltée.

# Table of Contents

| | |
|---|---:|
| Introduction | 9 |
| Notes to the Introduction | 34 |
| Antoine de Montchrestien, *Haman* | 37 |
| Anonymous, *New Tragedy of the Perfidy of Haman* | 87 |
| Notes | 110 |

# Acknowledgements

I would like to express my thanks to Paul Epstein and to Florence and Emmett Pybus for helping to make these translations more readable, to the editors of this series for their valuable comments and suggestions, to Shelley Kaplan who directed the New World premiere of *Perfidy of Haman*, and to Fran Mihura who so patiently assisted in the preparation of the typescript.

# Introduction

The present volume makes available for the first time to the English-speaking reader two of the most remarkable French plays based on the Bible, both derived from the Book of Esther. Montchrestien's *Aman* (*Haman*), one of the last French humanist tragedies, is also one of the most effective, containing passages of great poetic power.

It will be followed by a short pseudo-tragedy written by an unknown author and in mysterious circumstances. This undeservedly neglected spoof of serious drama ranks as one of the rare examples of Biblical farce that fully succeeds as entertainment without ever becoming offensive or irreverent.

That the tale of Esther and Haman proved especially fascinating to dramatists in France cannot be denied. In fact, during the period when tragedy was a flourishing genre in France (1550–1800), no fewer than ten tragedies appeared based on the Book of Esther, considerably more than on any other Old Testament story, and it was one of the most widely dramatized in other European countries, as well.

Why did this story attract so much attention? Perhaps it was simply the appeal of an exciting, somewhat melodramatic plot, complete with happy ending. It also lends itself equally well to a religious treatment (stressing the operation of divine providence) and to a secular treatment (focusing on the virtues and weaknesses of monarchs). At least three topical explanations might be offered, as well. 1) The theme of genocide (Haman's plot to exterminate the entire Jewish people) tended to assume special urgency at times of religious persecution, especially since Catholics and Protestants both identified with the beleaguered Jews in the Biblical narrative. Thus, Pierre Matthieu's three tragedies based on the Book of Esther date from the period of France's bloody religious civil wars; Pierre Du Ryer composed his version in the wake of Protestant uprisings during the 1620's, which were vigorously put down by Cardinal Richelieu; and Jean Racine wrote his only three years after the revocation of the Edict of Nantes, an action which essentially expelled all Protestants from the country. Racine presumably also had in mind the persecution, three decades earlier, of the Jansenist sect (in which he himself had been raised). 2) The presentation of a wicked minister and his deserved downfall likewise touched a responsive chord. The fact that many French tragedies from the seventeenth and eighteenth centuries featured kings' ministers as the villains probably reflected a desire on the part of many playwrights to criticize the government in power without directly linking the abuses to the monarch or even to the institution of monarchy. It was Pierre Corneille who most vividly illustrated the theory that kings are automatically endowed, through heredity, with heroic and virtuous instincts which they will naturally follow unless corrupted by vile counselors, usually of plebeian origin; but the basic outlines of that theory are visible in such earlier plays as Montchrestien's *Haman*. Moreover, the use of Biblical characters as a method of attacking powerful contemporaries was by no means limited to drama, and was especially common among Protestant polemicists of the late sixteenth century. 3) Esther is one of the rare heroines from antiquity who combines bravery with religious faith. At the same time, she lacks traits found in other frequently chosen heroines of tragedy that an austere Christian humanist might find troubling: that is to say, her triumph does not depend on seduction; her motives are primarily altruistic; she apparently never yields to passion; and she does not commit suicide.

## Haman

1. *The Author*

We possess only sketchy information about the life of Antoine de Montchrestien (1575?–1621).[1] He was born in the city of Falaise, in Normandy, probably between 1573 and 1576. (The uncertainty stems from the date of the portrait of Montchrestien which appeared in the 1601 edition of his plays, accompanied by the Roman numeral XXV. That has generally been assumed to represent the poet's age when the portrait was done, but the portrait itself is undated and may be somewhat earlier than 1601.) Tradition has it that his father was an apothecary, that the family name was originally Mauchrestien, and that the poet had no right to the particle "de" which he used in his signature. His parents, who died when he was quite young, must have been reasonably well-off, since Antoine later sued his guardian for misappropriating his heritage, and won. He attended a *collège*, probably at Caen, as companion to two young noblemen. Between 1601 and 1605 (biographers disagree on the year) he had to flee the country following a duel. He spent some time in Holland but he stayed in England for most of his exile. A copy of his tragedy about the death of Mary Stuart was presented to King James I, which quickly put the poet in that king's good graces. Thanks to James's personal intervention, Montchrestien was allowed to return to France, though again the date is uncertain. Having long since turned his back on letters, he went into business, first the manufacture of cutlery, and later a shipping venture, but neither proved very successful. In 1621 he joined the Huguenot revolt, in which he fought bravely. He was killed in a skirmish in the village of Tourailles, having achieved such notoriety as a rebel leader that the authorities had his dead body brought to Domfront, where it was broken on the wheel and burned.

Montchrestien's religious affiliation remains a matter of dispute. Some of his biographers claim that he was born a Catholic; others, a Protestant. He later married a Protestant woman and ended his life fighting for the Huguenot cause, but the former proves nothing, and his participation in the latter had more to do with ambition than with spiritual conviction. Nowhere in his plays does he expound and defend either religious viewpoint, even in *La Reine d'Ecosse*, where he had a perfect opportunity to do just that. He apparently favored religious toleration, although this is merely hinted at in his plays, and he was clearly an enthusiastic reader of the Bible.

We do not know why Montchrestien chose to abandon literature after 1604 when he was only in his late twenties or early thirties. Given his genuine poetic gifts and the scant achievements of his later years, we can only regret that decision. He left six tragedies, a pastoral play, a long narrative poem and a collection of lyric poetry, all published in the eight-year span from 1596 to 1604. In 1615 he published a book of a very different nature, a treatise on political economics, which has been called innovative for its time.

2. *A Non-Aristotelian Tragedy*

French tragedy is remembered today primarily for the great masterpieces of Corneille and Racine. It is rare to find a non-specialist, even in France, who has looked at any of the numerous tragedies produced during the nearly 100 years that preceded the advent of Corneille and the codification of the *doctrine classique* (the list of unities and precepts that French authors would consider as binding for two centuries). Although none of those plays qualifies as a masterpiece of the first rank, the best of them, including the tragedies of Montchrestien, can still be read with pleasure.

The origins of tragedy in France are directly linked to the humanist movement, which urged a radical break with the genres and conventions of the Middle Ages and, to take their place, the development of a brand new literature based on the Greek and Latin classics. The first French play to be called a tragedy was *Abraham sacrifiant* (1550) by Theodore de Bèze, one of the eminent figures of the Reformation. (It was performed in Lausanne, since the author had recently fled from France.) The first tragedy to be performed on French soil was *Cléopâtre captive* (1552) by Etienne Jodelle a member of the enormously influential group of young poets known as the Pléiade. The fact that a play by a nineteen-year-old poet could be staged before King Henri II and his court testifies to the esteem in which the humanists were held and served to inspire many other fledgling playwrights.

At the same time, this gala premiere signalled a decisive break between playwrights, audiences and actors. If the cast of *Cléopâtre captive* consisted of Jodelle and his friends, it was because existing companies of actors, whose repertory was drawn from the late medieval genres, such as mysteries, moralities, and farces were unprepared and probably unwilling to handle a radically different type of play. Apart from a few court performances, most humanist tragedies would be staged either by students in their schools or by semi-professional troupes comprised largely of older and former students in public squares. It is not until the closing years of the sixteenth century that we find an example of close contact between an author of tragedies and a competent professional troupe. Not surprisingly, the resumption of relations between playwrights and performers led to a far greater concern with stageworthiness. A parallel break between authors and audiences was even more inevitable, given the humanists' explicit aim of writing only for a highly erudite elite. A number of poets composed tragedies in Latin, and even those who wrote in French filled their plays with arcane mythological references, Latinate syntax, neologisms, and frequent allusions to or paraphrases of classical texts. While it is true that many of these plays received public performances which were well attended (of course, in that period public entertainments were far from plentiful), only a limited percentage of the audience could fully understand or appreciate them.

The most distinctive feature of the humanist tragedies is the absolute predominance of rhetorical set pieces, somewhat analogous to arias and duets in an opera. The authors' main objective was to display their virtuosity in extended lyrical solos, such as laments or ceremonial hymns, in eloquent debates between characters, and in overtly moralistic passages that restate commonplaces collected from ancient classics. Clearly, they derived their ideas on the nature of tragedy from sources other than Aristotle's *Poetics*. Indeed, there is no clear evidence that any French playwright or theorist knew Aristotle's treatise firsthand until the 1620's, even though it provoked endless discussions in Italy throughout the sixteenth century. The French humanists relied instead on Horace and a variety of classical grammarians and rhetoricians. For them, a tragedy was primarily a poem, and only secondarily a work for the stage. Moreover, since they viewed all poetry as a branch of epideictic, or demonstrative, rhetoric, poems needed to state arguments and to be persuasive. The preferred type of argument involved moral issues, and the poem as a whole had to be so effective as a tool of edification that it could not fail to have a beneficial impact on the reader. This theory, needless to say, attempted to counter the objection, raised as far back as Plato's *Republic*, that poetry does not make people morally better or promote the interests of society.

The French humanist view of tragedy differs from that of Aristotle in a number of key respects. First of all, plot is no longer central. The dramatic situation is chosen in view of the moral lesson it may teach and the rhetorical opportunities it provides. Unity of action was sometimes preserved but all too often ignored; it is not uncommon to find humanist tragedies with almost no action at all (for example, the action in all of Jodelle's *Cléopâtre captive* corresponds to the last scene in Shakespeare's *Antony and Cleopatra*), or too much (Garnier's *Antigone* covers the downfall of the entire family of Oedipus, moving from the wanderings of Oedipus to the combat of his two sons to the death of Antigone). Secondly, the playwrights preferred exemplary characters — in other words, general types as opposed to three-dimensional individuals. In many cases, characters are as starkly polarized as in melodrama, with flawless saints opposed to diabolical tyrants. Thirdly, while some plays (in accordance with Aristotle) feature as tragic hero a good man with a flaw or error in judgment, many humanist tragedies have as protagonist a Christian martyr whose heroic death inspires admiration (as in Montchrestien's *La Reine d'Ecosse*), a pagan knight who serves as a model of secular virtues (as in Montchrestien's *Hector*), or a despicable villain whose well-deserved death is an occasion for rejoicing (as in *Haman*). Finally, the notion of catharsis is absent. The tragic emotions, deemed to be pity and horror, were aroused through scenes of lamentation and through graphic descriptions of gruesome events. As in the case of *Haman*, those indispensable components do not necessarily occur during the final act, and unambiguously happy endings were allowed. The traditional image of the wheel of Fortune became inseparable from the humanist conception of tragedy, and thus any play that presented a powerful person's rise and fall, whether deserved or not, could with justification bear the label of tragedy.

The French humanists could find support for their non-Aristotelian views in the works of the most admired playwright of antiquity, Seneca.[2] That first-century Roman philosopher and poet, whose tragedies were far more influential than those of the Greeks, appealed to Renaissance tastes for the same reasons that cause most modern readers to dislike him: elaborate rhetorical display for its own sake, melodramatic characterization, an excess of violence and gore, and didactic passages promoting the stoic view of life. Seneca's larger than life heroes and villains speak and feel with an extreme intensity that makes the grandiloquent style seem appropriate. To be sure, Senecan tragedy had a major impact on the drama of other European countries during the Renaissance, but the imitation was probably most direct in France, where Seneca was not counterbalanced by other models.

Montchrestien, who was among the last French playwrights in the humanist tradition, was by no means an innovator. His plays provide a kind of summation of French dramatic accomplishments during the second half of the sixteenth century, without prefiguring what was to come next. If *Haman* displays the weaknesses of the humanist plays, it also possesses their strengths, especially the delight in vivid and richly textured poetic language, the ability to breathe new life into familiar stories and commonplaces, the intensity and range of emotions conveyed by the characters and the deep concern for moral and religious problems. Montchrestien's retelling of a popular Biblical narrative is no mere schoolboy exercise, but rather a meditation on human vanity and divine justice, possibly reflecting the author's own search for faith and his reactions to the violence and instability that he saw all around him.

## 3. *Staging*

Very little is known about the staging of French Renaissance plays. Indeed, at the beginning of this century scholars were claiming that only a handful of those works had ever been staged and that the authors did not compose their plays with performance in mind. Subsequently, both of those charges have been laid to rest. Yet, although we can confirm that many plays were acted in their authors' lifetimes, minimal information has surfaced about how they were performed.[3] It is certain that two of Montchrestien's tragedies received public performances. *Sophonisbe*, his first play, was acted by a group of university students at some point prior to the play's publication in 1596. *La Reine d'Ecosse* was staged by a troupe of strolling players on at least three separate occasions (in 1601, 1603, and 1604) and may conceivably have been revived in London at the court of King James I. There is no evidence that Montchrestien's other plays were performed, but the lack of documentation does not automatically prove that they were not. After all, we know of the performances of *La Reine d'Ecosse* only because they provoked a diplomatic incident. (The English ambassador to France objected to certain passages attacking Queen Elizabeth I, who was still on the throne, and asked the French authorities to ban the tragedy.) About the troupe that staged it, we know next to nothing. In fact, surprisingly little is known of the professional and semi-professional companies in sixteenth-century France. Thus, performance practice at the beginning of the seventeenth century is difficult to reconstruct. In all probability, there was little or no scenery except in elaborate court productions. The setting would have been vaguely suggested by a painted backdrop or a few columns. Since the actors probably stood as close as possible to the audience, there would have been no need for them to interact with the decor or even to call attention to its presence. In cases where the plot demands scene changes, it is unlikely that anything was done to modify the decor, even when the scene change occurs in the middle of an act. Every time one group of characters leaves and another group arrives, the audience would have to allow for the possibility that the scene has shifted.

Given the minimal amount of stage action in French humanist tragedy and the central position accorded to rhetorical display, it is likely that the actors moved around very little. They faced the audience rather than each other and used props only when absolutely necessary. That declamation was their primary function is clear even from the cast of character listings in the published versions of the plays in which the heading is more likely to be "Entreparleurs" (speakers) than "Acteurs." Audience and cast alike seemed to have conceived of a play, especially a tragedy, as an elaborate extension of the two most common rhetorical showcases, the formal oration and the debate, but delivered in costume and with more than the usual amount of gesture. Costumes were the most important accessory, indispensable to the creation of dramatic illusion. Of course, the richness and the historical accuracy of the costumes would depend on the means of the actors.

The static nature of these plays, with their excessively long speeches in heavily ornamented style, their paucity of action, and their overt moralizing, all of which makes them unpalatable to modern audiences, would not have been a drawback for the cultivated Renaissance spectator. Rhetorical display was heavily emphasized in the curriculum, and the practical value of proficiency in public speaking (especially for lawyers and statesmen) was one of the main reasons why so many sixteenth-century schoolmasters required their pupils to put on plays, either in Latin or in the vernacular. Humanist playwrights, moreover, generally agreed with Du Bellay that by writing plays modeled after those of ancient Greece and Rome, they were contributing to the collective enterprise of "illustrating" (i.e. making illustrious) the French language. Hence, it was primarily the poetic richness of their texts, and secondarily the moral edification (since Horace had prescribed for literature the dual purpose of delighting and teaching), by which the authors wished them to be judged. For all these reasons, what we today would call stageworthiness was never a major concern to the French humanists.

In an age when playwrights rarely tried to visualize the action as they wrote, Montchrestien's plays are better than average. His tragedies contain some theatrically effective scenes, especially the fast-moving fourth act of *Haman*, and he made a conscientious effort to show most of the action, rather than relegating virtually all of it to narrative passages, as was the case with many of his predecessors. Nevertheless, he could write entire acts in which there is no action at all (such as Act I of *Haman*); he is not always careful to indicate when characters enter or exit (for example, Mordecai suddenly speaks at the end of Act V, although no mention is made of when he came on stage); the identity of the character chorus is often unclear (in Act V the chorus that speaks at v. 1435 presumably consists of Persian courtiers, whereas the chorus that closes the act is composed of Jews); and in many instances we cannot be sure where the action is supposed to take place. Montchrestien probably gave little thought to such matters, but anyone wishing to stage the tragedy today would be obliged to work out some kind of solution. As the following chart should make clear, determining the setting of the various scenes of *Haman* is often a matter of conjecture:[4]

| Act I |  | Room in Haman's house or in the royal palace |
| Act II |  | Room in the royal palace |
| Act III | v. 607 | Square outside the palace |
|  | v. 741 | Esther's apartments |
|  | v. 871 | Square outside the palace, or Mordecai's house |
| Act IV |  | Throne room of the palace, with corridor adjacent to it |
| Act V | v. 1293 | Room in Haman's house |
|  | v. 1359 | Room in the royal palace |
|  | v. 1439 | Square outside the palace |
|  | v. 1491 | Esther's apartments |

Usually, we can figure out where the action is by noticing who is coming to visit whom: Haman calls on the king in Act II and in the second scene of Act V; Esther appears unsummoned before the king in Act IV; the king attends Esther's banquet in the final scene. That Act V begins in Haman's home is suggested by his account of encountering Mordecai upon leaving the palace (v. 1325) and by his wife's urging him to return to the king to obtain permission to raise a gallows (v. 1347). In all but one case (v. 741) Montchrestien marks a scene change within an act by bringing in the interlude chorus. The staging of Act III is the most problematic. At first reading one might assume that the act is playable on a single set, showing the square outside the palace and a balcony belonging to the queen's apartments. Esther would remain on the balcony while her emissaries descend to converse with Mordecai in the street below. However, Montchrestien gives no indication that the audience should see (in pantomime, presumably) the exchange between Mordecai, Sarah and Rachel during the queen's soliloquy, or that the queen should remain visible, though silent, during the exchanges between Mordecai and Hatach. Moreover, if Griffiths is right in assuming that the chorus of Jews that speaks at v. 871 is an interlude chorus (serving to mark a scene change), as well as a character chorus, then Mordecai must be presumed to have moved from the square where he was at the start of the act to some other unspecified location (perhaps his home). Nevertheless, there are problems with Griffiths's theory (namely, that the act contains only two scenes because the interlude chorus intervenes only once). If Esther can appear in the same spot as Mordecai (the square), even if he is assumed to have departed before she arrives, then she would have the right to leave and reenter the royal compound at will, rather than remain strictly guarded in a harem-like wing of the palace. But if the queen is able to leave her apartments as she pleases, then what would prevent her from going to speak to Mordecai in person, which would be more natural and more efficient? Why resort to the cumbersome process of sending messengers? For these reasons, I think a scene change must be supposed at v. 741, and the absence of the interlude chorus is an oversight on Montchrestien's part. Of course, the very fact that it is so hard to resolve these questions suggests that the playwright did not attach much importance to them. Like other French humanist dramatists, he tended to situate his characters in a vague and timeless rhetorical space, as opposed to the concrete and rigidly specified theatrical space which we have come to expect.

4. *Characterization*

Because Montchrestien follows the Book of Esther rather closely, his fleshing out of the main characters presents few surprises. Haman, of course, is arrogant, ruthless and vindictive. Moreover, since the Bible does not specify why he was elevated to the rank of prime minister, and since Montchrestien wanted to make the king appear just and competent, Haman is allowed some genuine merits: he has served with distinction as a military commander and has apparently discharged his ministerial duties conscientiously, at least prior to the start of the play. Ahasuerus has been purged of all his unseemly traits, especially his childish temper, his gluttony and drunkenness, and his lack of good judgment, as evidenced in the banquet episode. Montchrestien's decision to omit the first two chapters of the Book of Esther allows him to present Ahasuerus as a model ruler, serious-minded, fair and impervious to flattery. It is only by posing as a model of virtue that Haman can lead him astray. He displays more piety than in the Bible and also is far more demonstrative in his affection for Esther. The poet, by suppressing all mention of the previous queen and of the royal harem, presumably wanted his king to be more palatable to a Christian audience.

Following the example of Seneca and the other humanist playwrights, Montchrestien uses the soliloquy as one of his main techniques for revealing character. All three of the male principals in this play are introduced in a soliloquy. Even Esther, who is first shown in a dialogue with her two attendants, is granted a soliloquy only thirty lines after her initial entrance. In these passages the characters reveal their preoccupations and beliefs, as well as their personalities. The fact that each character gets multiple soliloquies allows the playwright to depict a greater range of emotional states and personality traits. Thus, Haman's opening speech displays his extreme arrogance; in Act II he challenges the Jewish God and all but deifies himself; in Act V he deplores his first major setback and comes to realize that his pride and excessive self-confidence were the product of bad judgment. Similarly, Esther's three soliloquies allow her to express her piety and courage in words as well as in deeds. Although she addresses God in all three of those speeches, they are not exclusively prayers. The queen also reflects on the vanity of earthly grandeur, her tenderness and concern for her uncle (Act III), her solidarity with her people, her belief both in an afterlife and in the manifestation of divine justice in this life (Act IV), and her confidence that God is directing her in the plan to save her people (Act V).

At times, due to Montchrestien's habit of conceiving each set piece in isolation, a character's tone and style may change abruptly from one scene to the next. Most notably, Ahasuerus, who appears as a calm and rational statesman in Act II, suddenly adopts the hyperbolic conceits of Petrarchan love poetry when describing his feelings for Esther in Act IV. However, these shifts are fewer in number and are less jarring than in some of Montchrestien's other tragedies (notably *Sophonisbe* and *David*). The characters seem basically consistent, and even Haman, the most complex character whose moods and tone change repeatedly during the play, remains fully credible.

## 5. *Argumentation*

If one of the salient characteristics of humanist tragedy is the frequency of long speeches and sustained debates, it is because the authors had much to say and took seriously the doctrine that literature must teach as well as please. The didactic intent is everywhere evident, often interfering with the flow of the action and not always perfectly integrated into the dramatic context. The presentation of timeless truths takes a variety of forms in these plays, none of them subtle but most playwrights of the era did not consider subtlety a virtue. However erudite the rest of their text might be, the moral lessons had to be easily grasped by all readers or viewers. Perhaps the most conspicuous of the localized didactic passages is the sentencia, or pithy moral maxim, which normally consists of only one or two lines.[5] Sententiae had been liberally used by Seneca, but Montchrestien and some of his French colleagues actually outdid the Latin dramatist in percentage of lines devoted to maxims. During the latter part of the sixteenth century it became customary to draw the reader's attention to the sententiae in books, including published versions of plays, by placing quotation marks in the left margin. This practice was followed in the 1604 edition of Montchrestien's plays, and the quotation marks have been retained for this translation. The sententiae in *Haman* consist of observations on a wide variety of topics, psychological and political, as well as moral and religious. The ideas are for the most part derived from Latin literature, with a smaller number based on the Bible or later Christian writers. Although this is technically a religious tragedy, secular maxims constitute a majority of the moral lessons, even those pronounced by the Jewish characters, reflecting both the humanist playwrights' reliance on Senecan models and Montchrestien's apparent fascination with the ethical teachings of stoicism.

Some of the maxims take on an ironic dimension when placed in the mouth of the villain. While Haman clearly enjoys posing as a virtuous man in order to impress the king, the audience is expected to see through his hypocrisy and to grasp both the truth of the statement and its inappropriateness to the speaker. Thus, for example, the maxim that wise rulers guard good men and punish the wicked (vv. 453–54) will later serve to justify Haman's execution, and his plea for mercy (vv. 1567–71) sounds hollow when compared to his earlier celebration of ruthlessness and vengeance. Haman's attempt to disprove the existence of God by denying the possibility of *creatio ex nihilo* (v. 548) and by debunking superstition (vv. 552–53) is likewise intended not to persuade the audience. At times the context makes a valid maxim seem comic, as when Haman ends a soliloquy of over sixty lines by justifying why he ought to stop speaking and begin to act (vv. 554–57)!

If the sententia is normally restricted to a few lines, choral interludes allow the humanist playwrights to moralize at great length.[6] They duly noted that Horace had declared in his *Ars poetica* that the chorus must favor the good characters, give sage counsel, praise such virtues as justice, moderation and peace, and implore heaven to punish wicked men and reward the good. He had also stated, in conformity with the practice of classical tragedy, that the chorus should function as an actor and converse with the solo characters, but, owing to a misprint in some Renaissance editions of Horace (reading "auctoris" for "actoris" in v. 193), many people understood him to mean that the chorus should take the part of the author and present the definitive commentary on the events within the play. Montchrestien uses the chorus at the end of acts, or at scene changes within acts to praise or denounce the characters and specify the appropriate moral lessons. This chorus, which

Griffiths terms the interlude or commentator chorus, exists outside of time and place, never interacting with the solo characters. It is not at all clear whether Montchrestien would have wanted it to remain present throughout the play; a modern director might opt to place the chorus on a platform overlooking the stage.

The utterances of the commentator chorus are always in strophic form, employing a considerable variety in the number and length of lines within a stanza. Although Renaissance writers knew that the choral episodes in classical tragedies were sung, it seems likely that they preferred to have the choruses in their own plays recited, for fear that music would render the words incomprehensible to the spectators and thus interfere with the moral lessons provided. The only clear-cut cases when we can be sure that the choruses were intended to be sung are the hymns in some of the early Protestant tragedies; it is possible that Montchrestien wanted the paraphrase of Psalm 124 at the end of *Haman* to be set to music, but we have no proof.[7] It could be argued that the authors who included sung choral passages with hymn-like texts were utilizing another form of didacticism by emphasizing the link between the story of the play and the audience's own religious beliefs. (There is also a second type of chorus, called by Griffiths the character chorus, that represents identifiable individuals, engages in dialogue with solo characters, and participates to some degree in the action. Some tragedies contain more than one character chorus; *La Reine d'Ecosse*, for example, features a group of Queen Elizabeth's counsellors and later a group of Mary's attendants. Montchrestien is usually careful to keep the two kinds of choruses distinct, though they apparently overlap in Act III of *Haman*.)

A more complex form of didacticism in *Haman* may be discovered by examining the tragedy as a whole, and in particular the balance between opposing characters and arguments. Every character is more than a mere individual; he or she also serves to articulate and defend a point of view, and possesses the requisite rhetorical ability to present it forcefully. However, the play is designed in such a way that one side is meant to emerge as clearly victorious. The villain, however eloquent, must fail to persuade the audience, and his ultimate downfall is supposed to signal a rejection of his views.[8] This pattern, which I have called the argumentative structure, means that both positions need to be argued at great length during the course of the play (Haman, for example, is allowed to blaspheme against God for over forty lines, and with a vehemence that would have been unthinkable in Racine's day), and that every point raised by the villain must be carefully rebutted by the good characters. It is significant that, although all French humanist tragedies contain lengthy debates, only a small percentage have an argumentative structure in which one point of view receives explicit endorsement; the convention is mostly confined to religious plays, in which characters take positions for or against God, and to polemical propaganda plays. Most of the time the authors did not consider themselves remiss if the various moral lessons contained within a play contradicted one another or were incompatible with their personal religious beliefs. They seemed to care even less about expressing a world view that would remain consistent from one play to the next. Instead, it often seems, as with Montchrestien, that the author simply adopted whatever moral views were found in the source he was reworking.[9] Nevertheless, even if it is impossible to determine Montchrestien's personal views with any certainty, he undeniably wished to make his *Haman* a pro-Biblical, pro-Christian play.

## 6. *The Two Versions of the Play*

The 1601 edition of Montchrestien's works contained six plays, namely, five tragedies and a pastoral. The 1604 edition, generally believed to be the last edition overseen by him, dropped the pastoral, added one new tragedy, *Hector*, and reprinted the five earlier tragedies in substantially revised form. The current translation uses the text of the later version.[10] Although nothing of substance was altered in the new version of *Haman*, Montchrestien shortened the play by exactly 100 lines and rewrote the majority of the remaining lines. The revisions are essentially stylistic in nature and rarely change the meaning significantly. Some of the modifications are so slight that they could not be reproduced in translation. As a typical example of stylistic revision, I give here a translation of the first six lines of the earlier version, to be compared with the text of the 1604 version later in this volume:

> Blond Phoebus, whether rising from the hollow
> Of the waves, to color the world's face anew,
> Or making the day flame with hotter rays
> Or going to lie down in the wet abode,
> Sees not one man in this habitable world
> Who in all happiness is comparable to me.

The cuts are mostly short, rarely consisting of more than four lines. The main exceptions are Esther's monologue at the start of

Act IV, which is shortened from 52 lines to 32, and the king's speech following it, cut from 38 lines to 10. In the queen's prayer we lose nothing but a fuller elaboration of what she is asking God to do on her people's behalf. The revision of the king's speech, however, involves changes in staging and mood. In the 1601 version, Ahasuerus, having just glimpsed Esther through the window before her arrival in the throne room, waxes ecstatic over her loveliness. Because the later version has the queen enter the throne room immediately following the close of her monologue and eliminates mention of the window, the king first sees her from the back of the room and has much less time to describe her beauty. Here is the portion of the speech which Montchrestien later deleted, revealing him to be an able practitioner of the type of love poetry perfected by the Pléiade:

> 1230 Venus herself would not equal her walk;
> Although the face of majesty is such
> That it's grave and severe, as well as sweet and fair.
> Truly, I think that her eyes' shining rays
> Could not but make the sun turn envious
> 1235 And that, ashamed to have a lesser light,
> He often hides him in the ocean's waves.
> These are no eyes, but rather gleaming stars,
> Producing in my heart happiness or woe;
> With just one glance they make me live or die,
> 1240 And with just one lure force me to follow them.
> In short, holding my heart in their fair prison,
> They now control my reason as they please.
> Forever blessed be that immortal Model
> From whence this fair Grace came into the world,
> 1245 A Grace who, playing, can surmount hearts, can
> Conquer the bravest conquerors with no effort.
> Besides, all the perfumes with which Assyria
> Teems do not smell as good as her breath does.
> Also, her lovely mouth reveals when smiling
> 1250 Two perfectly matched rows of Orient's pearls;
> The coral, too, that keeps these pearls enclosed
> Shames the red hue of the reddest roses. Also,
> Her gentle greeting could calm even Mars
> When he, amidst his soldiers, seethes with anger.
> 1255 So many beauties does her soul conceal
> That mortals all judge her to be immortal.
> Did I not act well by deposing Vashti,
> Since I've acquired such a treasure for myself?

A modern reader might object that the tone of this speech does not fit in with the rest of the play, but the poetry is pleasing, and the hyperbolic language may help to explain why the king accedes so readily to Esther's requests. Because Montchrestien's principal concern in preparing the revised version of his play was to improve the style, he did not reread the Book of Esther. On three occasions he changed the text without realizing that the revision no longer conforms to the Bible. Thus, in v. 341 Ahasuerus states that his empire comprises 122 provinces, rather than the Bible's 127; the 1601 version had read simply "so many, many provinces" (v. 353). Likewise, Zeresh tells her husband in the earlier version to erect a gallow fifty cubits high, as in the Bible (v. 1435); Montchrestien altered this to thirty cubits in the revised version (v. 1343). The most puzzling alteration occurs during the final scene. The queen, after denouncing Haman and his extermination order, reveals for the first time that she is a Jewess and related to Mordecai. In the 1601 text she conveys that vital information in the following lines: "For this benevolent, obliging nation / Gave to us both our name and origin" (vv. 1639–40). The 1604 version alters the second line to read "Gives us our name and origin, as you know" (v. 1540). The seemingly innocuous filler "as you know" makes nonsense of the situation, since, if Ahasuerus had indeed known that his beloved wife was Jewish, he would never have gone along with Haman's scheme. In these passages the current translation has preferred the text of the 1601 edition.

Among the other changes made in 1604, Montchrestien dropped the subtitles for all his tragedies (this play was first entitled *Haman* or *Vanity*). The new edition, as already mentioned, adds hundreds of quotation marks to set off the sententiae within the plays. Harder to explain is the elimination of the "Entreparleurs" (cast of characters) listing, restored in this translation. In the 1604 text, each act is prefaced by a list of the characters who appear in it, but in three cases out of five that list is incomplete. One result is that we never learn the full name of Haman's confidant, who is designated only by the letters Ri. In the earlier version he bears the name Cirus, and I have followed the example of the Petit de Julleville edition by retaining that name.

## 7. *Sources*

The principal source is the Book of Esther, including the six and a half supplementary chapters included in Catholic Bibles (but relegated in

Protestant and Jewish Bibles to the collection of non-canonical works, or Apocrypha). The tragedy contains paraphrases of two psalms, and there are numerous Biblical echoes, the most significant of which will be pointed out in the Notes. There is no evidence that Montchrestien was familiar with earlier French plays on the subject, though he may have known the neo-Latin play of the same name by Claude Roillet. If so, he imitated only the structure of the earlier play, but virtually nothing of its content. (Roillet's first act consists of a conversation between Haman and a moralizing old man, followed by Haman's interview with the king. Act II begins with Mordecai's soliloquy, continues with the exchange of messages between him and Esther, and ends with a prayer for Mordecai and the chorus. Act III begins with Esther's prayer, after which point the two plays diverge.) At most Roillet helped Montchrestien by showing how to compress the action and where to place major set pieces. As for the tragedies composed in French, André de Rivaudeau's *Aman* (1566) and Pierre Matthieu's *Esther* (1585), later expanded into two plays *Vasthi* and *Aman* (1589), there is no clear evidence that they influenced Montchrestien, although it is conceivable that he may have read them.

Montchrestien's tragedy contains a number of mythological references, carefully confined to the non-Jewish characters and relatively few in number. Not surprisingly, there are also extensive allusions to Latin authors, especially Seneca, who furnished stylistic techniques as well as moral lessons. For example, the chorus's condemnation of anger in Act II is in its broad outlines inspired by Seneca's *De Ira*. More often the borrowing is brief, with the original somewhat altered. Thus, Cyrus's observation that "One can change countries but not one's own nature" (v. 177) is borrowed from Horace's *Epistles* (I.11.27): "They change their climate, not their disposition, who run beyond the sea." Likewise, the passage in Mordecai's third-act soliloquy where he calls those who died fighting for Jerusalem "three and four times happy" is a reminiscence of speeches in the *Odyssey* (V. 306 ff) and the *Aeneid* (I. 94 ff). Given the considerable differences between the religion of the classical pagan authors and that of the Old Testament, Montchrestien shows genuine artistry in harmonizing his borrowings from the two sets of sources.

8. *Note on the Translation*

I have rendered the alexandrines as iambic pentameter and have not attempted to reproduce the rhyming couplets of the original or the special rhyme schemes found in the choruses (AABBA in Act I, ABAB in Act II, AABBCC in Act III, ABBACC in Act IV, AABCCB in Act V) or in Mordecai's hymn (ABAB). I have tried to make the translation both as faithful and as readable as possible; I would hope that it is sufficiently stageworthy to be used for performance (although huge cuts would be required for the sake of a contemporary audience). With only rare exceptions I have avoided stilted poetic forms, and I have chosen not to use the archaic pronouns "thou" and "thee." I have added stage directions for the reader's convenience; the original has none at all.

## New Tragedy of the *Perfidy of Haman*

### 1. *Date and Authorship*

One of the most mysterious works in the history of French drama is an anonymous play published in 1622 under the title *Tragédie nouvelle de la Perfidie d'Aman*. It bears no resemblance to any other French Biblical play, and its authorship seems impossible to determine. Its principal innovations are the total absence of moral didacticism or religious edification, the farcical tone maintained through much of the play, a sizable amount of literary parody, and an unusual degree of freedom in handling the Biblical narrative. Especially atypical of French dramatic practice is the insertion of a virtually unrelated comic interlude placed between the second and third acts.

Performance information must be deduced from a little farce printed in the same volume with *Perfidy of Haman*. It too is anonymous (the title page states merely that it is the product of "one of the gentlest wits of the age"). However, the names of two of the characters reveal not only that the farce was performed, but by which troupe. Turlupin and Gros-Guillaume (Fat Bill) were the stage names of two of the most renowned comic actors of that generation, Henri Legrand and Robert Guérin, who, after many years of performing comic playlets and monologues with a third actor, Hugues Guéru, joined forces in the fall of 1622 with the Comédiens du Roi. This troupe, better known as the Hôtel de Bourgogne (the name of the hall in Paris in which they normally played), had just returned to make its long-desired "comeback" in the capital and took out a lease on their hall beginning October 6 of that year.[11]

Since the parts of Turlupin and Gros-Guillaume must have been written for Legrand and Guérin, and since no one else would have played them while these stars were still active, we must conclude that the farce was performed by the Comédiens du Roi in the final months of 1622. Given the perennial popularity of these actors, any farce written for them would presumably be performed. In fact, in light of the theatrical conventions of the period, the printing of the farce testifies to its success.

That *Perfidy of Haman* was also in their repertory can be affirmed from the coexistence of the two plays in the same volume with continuous pagination and with both listed on the title page. It is also evident, in light of the fierce rivalry between troupes in the seventeenth century, that the Comédiens du Roi would not allow a farce of theirs to be printed with a play from another company.

Since the eighteenth century it has been traditional for drama historians to label this pseudo-tragedy as one of the numerous polemical pieces surrounding the downfall and assassination of the Maréchal d'Ancre in 1617. That hypothesis is no longer tenable today. It rests on the supposed existence of an earlier edition in 1617, yet no trace has ever been found of such an edition, and it is doubtful that there ever was one.[12]

The alleged polemical intent of the play is also undercut by the lack of recognizable references to the Maréchal and by the fact that those few passages which may contain topical allusions do not fit his biography. For example, Mordecai alleges in Act II that Haman is of plebeian origin, that he earlier worked as a "planeur" and that his father was a dressmaker ("couturier"). However, we know that Concino Concini came from a well-connected, if not an aristocratic family. While his father rose no higher than notary to the city of Florence, his grandfather had been minister of state under Grand Duke Cosimo de' Medici. Moreover, Concini's assassination in 1617 provoked a series of polemical poems and pamphlets, one of which was in play form. If *Perfidy of Haman* were indeed composed in that year, it should have contained references to the major grievances against the highly unpopular minister, such as his foreign birth, his incompetence in affairs of state, his deliberate alienation of the nobility, and most of all, resentment of his even more powerful wife Leonora, who had long been the Queen Mother's chief confidante. Incidentally, Leonora, who was convicted of sorcery and executed shortly after her husband, also occasioned a number of polemics, including a play entitled *La Magicienne étrangère*. Yet Haman's wife is not even mentioned until the final lines of the play, and we learn nothing about her except that she exists.

Again, the play mentions a popular uprising, but it is never connected with Haman and occurs prior to his arrest; yet a play written in 1617 could not have failed to make an explicit connection with the gruesome riot in which Concini's body was exhumed by an enraged mob, mutilated and paraded through the streets of Paris. In the final analysis, the only genuine similarities between *Perfidy of Haman* and the historical Concini are the ministers' vanity and arrogance, the fact that both were overthrown and executed on the same day, and the use of a gallows.[13]

The near certainty that the play was publicly performed in 1622 also renders the polemical hypothesis unlikely. The Maréchal had been a protégé of Maria de' Medici, who had fled from Paris shortly after his assassination and became reconciled to her son Louis XIII in 1621. It is simply inconceivable that the authorities would permit the public performance in Paris of a play that purported to satirize the Maréchal so soon after the Queen Mother's return. Moreover, as the opening speech of the play unmistakably shows, the King is portrayed in just as ridiculous a light as Haman, which means that if the work was intended as a political satire, Louis XIII would become one of its targets. No troupe would dare caricature a reigning monarch, especially a newly arrived troupe seeking a permanent home in Paris.

The play itself probably contains certain clues about its origin, but they are too vague to yield any substantive information. For example, reference is made in Act III to an uprising in a provincial town, facetiously named Esdron (probably suggesting Estron, i.e. excrement). But the reign of Louis XIII was a period of great agitation, and there are numerous instances of peasant revolts and of insurgencies led by disgruntled noblemen. The allusion is not detailed enough to permit a precise identification. Likewise, the Executioner's remark that Haman will have to spend the rest of the winter on the gallows (v. 578) suggests that the first performance occurred in midwinter. Which winter is impossible to determine.

2. *Use of Sources*

While any Biblical play is bound to deviate from the original story, at least to some slight degree, *Perfidy of Haman* takes more sweeping liberties with its sources than any other Esther play. Indeed, one would be hard pressed to cite another example of a play with such cavalier treatment of the Bible.

Among the minor discrepancies between source and play, we should note that according to the Bible, Zethar and Harbona are two of the king's chamberlains, not princes; the Jews have been living in Shushan for considerably more than one year, contrary to Esther's assertion (v. 169); Haman is not described as a military commander (v. 287; perhaps the author derived this detail from Montchrestien's tragedy); the king orders his chronicles to be read to him in the middle of the night because he is unable to sleep, whereas in the play he gives this order in the daytime and for no apparent reason (v. 432); it is Harbona, not Zethar, who informs the king that Haman has built a gallows for Mordecai (vv. 543–44); it is not until the king has left the room that Haman falls at Esther's feet and pleads for mercy, whereas in the play the king remains and it is unclear why Haman should direct his entreaties to the queen (vv. 549–50).

The more serious discrepancies concern the timing of the various events and the causal relations between them. For example, the king's banquet appears to be going on throughout the three acts of the play, although in the Bible the coronation of Esther and the promotion of Haman take place some time after the conclusion of the grandiose six-month celebration. In fact, the conversation between the king and his princes in Act I suggests that the banquet has only been in progress for a short while. The play does not explain how Esther was chosen to replace Vashti, and it gives the impression that she has not yet been made queen (v. 109). There is no danger involved in Esther's appearing before the king without being summoned, which she does twice in the play. Perhaps the most puzzling feature of her role in the play is that she invites Ahasuerus and Haman to a private supper in her apartments while the main banquet is still in progress; then everyone forgets about her invitation, and Esther has to make a second appearance at the king's banquet to plead for her people, whom she unaccountably fails to name! Moreover, if the point of inviting Haman is to accuse him in person, why does she not wait to plead her case until Haman returns to the palace at v. 537?

The role of Mordecai has been altered beyond recognition. Instead of the stern patriarch who lectures Esther about her duty to her God and her people, the playwright makes him a figure of farce who insults Haman to his face, believes he can get away with anything because of his kinship to the queen, and never even mentions the imminent danger facing his people. In fact, the play establishes no link between Haman's hatred of Mordecai and the order to exterminate the Jews.

Even more strangely, the king seems unaware of that decree, since Haman presumably used the royal seal without permission when he promulgated it (v. 534). Moreover, Haman does not seem to need the king's permission to hang Mordecai on a private gallows, whereas in the Bible the minister's appearance at court at daybreak in order to obtain that permission allows him to be present at the very moment when Ahasuerus, having heard the reading from his chronicles, has just decided to bestow a special honor upon Mordecai.

The anonymous playwright did not limit himself to altering his source; he also inserted wholly new characters and scenes. The four invented characters are all delightfully comic: the devil Duranda, who has escaped from Hades and taken up residence with Haman because the latter feeds his staff so much better; the two farcically named servants who steal food and wine from the royal banquet; and the wise-cracking executioner who taunts Haman in the final scene. There are also new episodes involving non-invented characters, such as the king's boasting speech, the confrontation between Mordecai and Haman, and the discussion of a riot in a provincial town. All these passages are at best loosely integrated into the plot, so that the play seems to be little more than a succession of amusing scenes, with frequent references to food and gluttony.

Given the magnitude of these changes, we are entitled to wonder whether the playwright made them deliberately, or whether they result from haste, carelessness, or even ignorance. If we suppose ignorance as the cause, then why did the author select a plot from a source he hardly knew? If, on the other hand, he had a thorough acquaintance with the Book of Esther, why would he go out of his way to make the story line obscure and to add so many farcical scenes to it? There is no certain answer to these questions, although I shall formulate my own hypothesis in the following section.

It is conceivable, though by no means certain, that the mysterious playwright might have known one of the earlier French dramatizations of the Esther story. The *Mystere du Viel Testament* (middle of the fifteenth century) has two lengthy comic scenes featuring the executioner Gournay and his inept assistant Micet, who are ordered to hang first the pair of treacherous eunuchs, and later their boss, the provost Aman. Yet there are no close resemblances between those passages and the final scene of *Perfidy of Haman*. In fact, Gournay in the earlier play treats the condemned Aman with respect, asking his forgiveness for what he is required to do, and urging him to resign himself to his fate and pray to the gods. Another possible source is Montchrestien's tragedy, in which the haughty minister claims in considerable detail to have achieved distinction as a military commander, and the accuracy of this boast is never questioned. Yet in *Perfidy of Haman* the claim to military prowess is confined to a single line (v. 287) within a hyperbolic speech of self-glorification, and it is treated as an unimportant detail.

If the playwright's attitude toward the Bible was playful, his use of conventions from French tragedy of the late sixteenth century, which he seemed to know quite well, is nothing short of parodic. Despite the word "tragedy" in its title, *Perfidy of Haman* contains only one thoroughly serious scene, which is the queen's prayer. Moreover, the opening line of Haman's boasting speech, "Peer to the King I walk," is a deliberate echo of the opening line of a similar speech in Robert Garnier's *Les Juives* (1587), where Nebuchadnezzar had proclaimed, "Peer to the gods I walk" (v. 279), itself based on a speech from Seneca's *Thyestes* (v. 885). Other conventions parodied in this pseudo-tragedy include the use of quotation marks to call sententiae to the reader's attention (vv. 139–40), the rhetorical device of adunaton, or listing of impossibilities (vv. 46–52), the suggestion that an unfeeling man must have been suckled by a tiger (v. 135), the lengthy description of Esther's physical beauty (v. 111–26) (Montchrestien had placed an analogous passage in the mouth of the king in the 1601 version of his *Haman*, (vv. 1225–56)), discussion of the fickle goddess Fortune and her wheel (vv. 591–94), desire for the restoration of the legendary golden age (vv. 426–31), and the constant use of mythological names, including the substitution of the name of a god for the god's specialty ("Thetis" to refer to the sea in v. 15, "Bacchus" for wine in v. 88, "Bellona" for war in v. 136, "Phoebus" for sun in v. 503; these have not been maintained in the present translation).

The author's favorite techniques of deflation are the abrupt change from elevated to colloquial style, sometimes occurring within the same speech (notably at vv. 37, 197, 305); the confrontation between the pompous character using lofty diction (Haman) and an opponent who uses coarse language and insults him to his face (Mordecai, the Executioner); the puns and other humorous remarks; the frequent references to eating and drinking activities normally considered too undignified to be shown in a French tragedy; and the jaunty, conversational pace of most of the dialogue, in stark contrast to the stately and highly ornate speech found in sixteenth-century tragedies.

## 3. A New Hypothesis

It is tantalizing to speculate that *Perfidy of Haman* was adapted from an early Purimspiel, now lost. The fact that so much farce has been added to the story, with special emphasis on food and gluttony in every scene, would at the very least make it suitable for use on the Jewish festival of Purim. It is also noteworthy that Esther's prayer (the only speech where the Jewish God is named) is not at all based on Chapter 14 of the apocryphal portion of the Book of Esther, which was normally drawn upon by Christian playwrights treating the Esther story.

On the other hand, it is clear that the text as it was printed in 1622 is not of Jewish authorship. The curious discrepancies between the play and the Biblical account suggest a limited familiarity with the Book of Esther, while the parody of French humanist drama indicates acquaintance with the Pléiade and their followers, as well as Rabelais. There is no single passage that gives clear evidence of a Jewish playwright. Moreover, although we know that Jewish communities in several European countries were in the habit of producing plays, no records have come to light of any Purimspiel tradition in France. The fact that Louis XIII had promulgated an edict of expulsion against the Jews in 1615, confirming earlier decrees dating back to 1306, would not have made this a propitious moment for the creation of Jewish drama.

A possible solution to this difficulty is to assume that the French author, whose knowledge of the Old Testament was minimal, was adapting an Italian Purimspiel, of which he possessed only a scenario or an abbreviated text. Although it must be acknowledged that only a handful of Italian Jewish plays from the sixteenth century are still extant, none of which is a possible source for *Perfidy of Haman*, several of the play's peculiarities lend support to the assumption of an Italian connection. Between the second and third acts is a farcical interlude with minimal connection to the rest of the play. The use of intermezzi between the acts of a serious play or opera was quite common in Italy during this period, whereas in France they were a rarity, found only in a small number of court productions. Likewise, the convention of including farcical characters and scenes within a tragedy was well established in Italy, but not in France, where such mingling of genres was rarely found outside of tragicomedies. Finally, there is a possibility that the farce published together with *Perfidy of Haman* was composed under Italian influence. Gustave Lanson, who first proposed that theory, noted that this playlet, unlike other French farces, is written in prose, and that the father embarks on one of his ships for the Indies, which would be a more likely destination for a Venetian than for a French merchant.[14]

In the final analysis, it seems impossible to determine why the play was written, or by whom, or how successful it was. It was never reprinted, and there have been no known revivals until the New World premiere, produced by me and using this translation, in March of 1980 at the University of Chicago.

## 4. *The Translation*

I have done my best to give a clear and faithful rendering of a text that is at times very corrupt. The frequently incoherent punctuation has been carefully corrected. I have used the standard English spelling for the names of characters who are mentioned in the Bible. For several of the other characters, I have had to make choices since there are discrepancies between the names in the Cast of Characters and those in the text of the play. The devil is called Durandal in the cast listing and Duranda in Act II. As for the two farcical servants, I have rendered Happe-souppe as Snatch-soup. (As a hyphenated noun, it meant "spoon.") His comrade is called Frippe-sausse ("lick-dish" is one of the equivalents in Cotgrave's dictionary; the name is borrowed from Rabelais) in the cast listing, but appears later under the name Guingnotrou ("peek in the hole"). Stage directions have been added for the reader's convenience; the original gives only one, noting Haman's entrance at v. 279.

## NOTES TO INTRODUCTION

1. For the most recent update on Montchrestien's biography, see Michael Paulson, "New Light on the Life and Works of Montchrestien" in *Papers in Romance* Vol. 3 No. 3 (1981), 153–59.
2. For an in-depth study of Senecan influence on French and English Renaissance tragedy, see Gordon Braden, *Renaissance Tragedy and the Senecan Tradition* (New Haven and London: Yale University Press, 1985).
3. On the question of staging, see Eugène Rigal, *De Jodelle à Molière* (Geneva: Slatkine, 1969; reprint of Paris, 1911); Richard Griffiths, *The Dramatic Technique of Antoine de Montchrestien* (Oxford: Clarendon Press, 1970) pp. 146–58, which remains the definitive study of this playwright.
4. My reconstruction is somewhat closer to that of Griffiths than to that of George Otto Seiver in his critical edition of *Aman* (Philadelphia: University of Pennsylvania Press, 1939) pp. 15–24. Seiver, who defends the play's stageworthiness, proposes a simplified version of the compartment stage as found in the *Mémoire de Mahelot*: The king's apartments are on one side of the stage, the queen's are on the other side, and all the other episodes would be played in the neutral area at the center of the stage. His analysis, although detailed, never really addresses the knottiest problems.
5. An entire volume was devoted to the use of this rhetorical device: Paul Kahnt, *Gedankenkreis der Sentenzen in Jodelle's und Garnier's Tragödien und Seneca's Einfluss auf denselben* (Marburg: H. G. Elwert, 1887). For a brief overview, see Jacques Scherer, *La Dramaturgie classique en France* (Paris: Nizet, 1968) pp. 316–32; and Griffiths, pp. 96–105.
6. Cf. Griffiths, pp. 138–45. See also my article "The Didactic Chorus in French Humanist Tragedy" in *Classical and Modern Literature* Vol. 3 No. 3 (1983), 139–49.
7. For fuller treatment of this question, see Helen M. C. Purkis, "Choeurs chantés ou parlés dans la tragédie française au XVIe siècle" in *Bibliothèque d'Humanisme et Renaissance* 22 (1960), 294–301.
8. See my article "Good and Evil Heroes in the Tragic Theatre of Antoine de Montchrestien" in *Bibliothèque d'Humanisme et Renaissance* 40 (1978), 575–81.
9. The consensus among present-day scholars is that Montchrestien had no clearly definable philosophical position. The most important statement of the opposing view is Kurt Willner, *Montchrestiens Tragödien und die stoische Lebensweisheit* (Berlin: E. Ebering, 1932).
10. *Haman* was published five times during the seventeenth century, but there are actually only two versions, since the 1603 edition is an exact reprint of the 1601 text; the 1606 edition reprints the 1604 text, reproducing all the old errors and adding new ones; and the 1627 (posthumous) edition

reproduces the 1601 text with insignificant variants, even though it also includes the prefatory material of the 1604 text. For an exhaustive comparison of the different versions, see the introduction to Seiver's critical edition, pp. 4–15. The precise dating of the original edition is somewhat unclear, since the title page bears no date, and the two prefatory pieces which feature the date 1601 appear to have been added after the rest of the volume had been printed (see Paulson, p. 154).

11 See Sophie-Wilma Deierkauf-Holsboer, *Le Théâtre de l'Hôtel de Bourgogne* (Paris: Nizet, 1968), Vol. I, Chapter 6.

12 For a fuller discussion, see Henry Carrington Lancaster, *A History of French Dramatic Literature in the Seventeenth Century* (Baltimore: Johns Hopkins University Press, 1929–42) I, 185–86.

13 See M. Chanoine-Davranches, "Le Maréchal et la marquise d'Ancre: l'histoire et les pamphlets" in *Précis analytique des Travaux de l'Académie des sciences, belles-lettres et arts de Rouen*, 1910–11, 213–392.

14 See Lancaster, I, 218.

## BIBLIOGRAPHY

Besides the works mentioned in the notes to the introduction, the following works on Montchrestien and early French tragedy are important sources of historical information and reference material.

Bray, R., *La Formation de la doctrine classique en France*. Paris, 1926.

Charpentier, F., "Le Thème d'Aman et la propagande huguenote." *Bibliothèque d'Humanisme et Renaissance*, 33 (1971), 377–83.

Dabney, L., *French Dramatic Literature in the Reign of Henri IV*. Austin, Texas, 1952.

Forsyth, E., *La Tragédie française de Jodelle à Corneille: le thème de la vengeance*. Paris, 1962.

Lanson, G., *Esquisse d'une histoire de la tragédie en France*. New York, 1920.

Lawton, H., *A Handbook of French Renaissance Dramatic Theory*. Manchester, 1949.

Lebègue, R., *La Tragédie française de la Renaissance*. Brussels, 1954.

―――――― , *La Tragédie religieuse en France: les débuts*. Paris, 1929.

Loukovitch, K., *L'Evolution de la tragédie religieuse classique en France*. Paris, 1933.

Seidmann, D., *La Bible dans les tragédies religieuses de Garnier et de Montchrestien*. Paris, 1971.

Stone, D., *French Humanist Tragedy: A Reassessment*. Manchester, 1974.

# HAMAN

Antoine de Montchrestien

## Cast of Characters

(in order of appearance)

| | |
|---|---|
| HAMAN | prime minister of the Persian empire |
| CYRUS | his friend |
| KING AHASUERUS | |
| MORDECAI | uncle to the queen |
| SARAH | attendant to the queen |
| RACHEL | attendant to the queen |
| QUEEN ESTHER | |
| HATACH | the queen's eunuch |
| ARPHAXAT | attendant to the king |
| ZERESH | Haman's wife |
| MESSENGER | |
| CHORUSES | (of Courtiers, Jews, Timeless Observers) |

# ACT I

*(Enter Haman and Cyrus.)*

Haman:  Kind Phoebus, whether rising from the waves
At dawn to give fair daylight to the world,
Or blazing forth with hotter rays at noon,
Or plunging back into the chilly sea,
Spies no one man in this habitable globe     5
Who by his happy lot compares to me.
My glory's peerless; if one of the gods,
In love with earth, chose to desert the skies,
To live in lesser greatness 'neath the moon,
He might well be content with my high fortune.     10
The whole world fears my prince, obeys his law,
And he wishes no other friend but me:
In all he graciously defers to my advice,
In fact I'm king; I do not bear the title,
But tush! it's just the same; for the name fits     15
Him who does all he says, says all he wants.
Must a host of warriors be sent to the field
To subdue the universe by force of arms?
Must we strike terror into the most daring
And kindle fury in the coldest hearts?     20
Must an important matter be resolved at once?
These weighty burdens fall to me alone.
Thus when amid the warriors I advance,
Palm crowns and laurels mingle on my brow;
Then when by me peace is restored to earth,     25
My head is crowned with wreaths of olive branches.
As I bear, both in war and peace, unwearied,
The burdens of a state that would tire Atlas,[1]

Thus with the crown of my head I touch heaven,
And never shall fear that its angry tempest
Will hurl me to the ground with thunderbolts.
Those on whom destiny bestowed my good luck,
Exalting them so high above the common rabble,
Are safely lodged, sheltered from fortune's blows.
All things work in their favor; when they spread
Their nets, they catch cities and towns in plenty.
"O thrice and four times happy can the man be
"Called, who sees gods and men smile on his plans,
"And who has no sooner wished a thing to happen
"Than the happy outcome satisfies his wish.
I, for one, never undertook a project
That did not come itself to meet my goal.
And you're my witness, you who in many dangers
Saw how I crushed the pride of foreign peoples,
Who, boiling with heroic zeal in combat,
Came to know my fortune and my valiant hand.
How many diverse times in such diverse places
Did you see dusty fields covered with carnage
By this formidable sword, and bloody streams
Drag off the stinking corpses by the thousands?[2]

Cyrus: On that account I feel covered with glory,
To have followed your victorious camp each place;
For though your honor stays beyond compare,
And though there's no one in your league but you,
We others, following your laurel's shadow,
Still hold a rank above all other warriors,
And we're esteemed by foreign nations to
The degree your praises swagger over us.
Now who could number all the hostile armies
Whom just the news of your strength put to flight;
How many times your single courage won
Battles, scaled ramparts, and broke through defenses,
Made peoples tribute to your unconquered king?
'Twould be like counting ears of grain in summer,
Sweet fruits in autumn, icicles in winter,
And the diverse flowers with which April's crowned.

Haman: It's thanks to you, my noble-hearted comrades,
That I'm esteemed to be so great and valiant.

              Magnanimous, invincible men of war,
              If I rise to heaven, my wings are your weapons.       70
              Through them do I become a peerless eagle
              Who without blinking can behold our sun.
              If your sight still is dazzled totally
              By its bright light, making you cast your eyes down,
              "Don't be astonished. Human greatness comes           75
              "To full perfection through discrete advances.
              "The fertile fruit trees, when the spring comes, push
              "A sweet and lovely flower out of its cover:
              "It sets into fruit; summer comes to nourish it,
              "And autumn following makes the greenness ripen:      80
              "Likewise, in one's fortune one must wait for time,
              "And by degrees time can perfect it. All
              "Is done through seasons; he who wants to do well
              "Must in no way upset the established order.³
              You see how time has made me such a great man,        85
              How I am called a miracle throughout
              The earth, from the pearly shore where the sun rises,
              To the Spanish sea where its repose takes place.
              Now, of all the exploits that enshrine my glory
              In the eternal rolls in Memory's Temple,              90
              Although by reason they are mostly mine,
              Yet I must grant a part of them to chance,
              But still more to you, invincible men of war,
              Who, sweating with me 'neath the weight of armor,
              Made known to those who've met you in the field       95
              That for you alone the impossible is possible.
              I therefore deem the glory of battles shared
              Between me foremost and you all and fortune.
              But all this good advice, which visibly
              Keeps so many subject peoples dutiful,                100
              So many provinces calm and well-ordered,
              At least, without envy, will be my sole trophy.
Cyrus:        Throughout the wide world it's known that you make
              Both war and peace, just as it pleases you.
              That's why the best men reverence you sincerely,      105
              And even the wicked do so with constraint,
              By law commanded to adore you humbly.
Haman:        If my king wants to honor me so greatly,

|  | If to my prowess he pays that deserved reward, |  |
|  | Well, I must try my hand in seeking vengeance. | 110 |
|  | But he who wants with ostentatious pride to |  |
|  | Defy me must be punished for presumption. |  |
|  | "Whoever wants to remove honor from virtue |  |
|  | "Aims to deprive it of its own reward; |  |
|  | "And if this virtue were left without praise, | 115 |
|  | "You'd see great hearts lose eagerness for it. |  |
| Cyrus: | Could someone dare to give you such an insult? |  |
|  | Adorned by gifts of heaven, nature's graces |  |
|  | And royal favors, all in competition, |  |
|  | You must excite the gods alone to envy. | 120 |
|  | Your glory is too bright, too fully fueled. |  |
|  | "No smoke comes from a clear and shining flame. |  |
| Haman: | "No greatness truly great is without envy. |  |
|  | "Nobles are always hateful to their subjects; |  |
|  | "And those favored by fortune and the king | 125 |
|  | "Are commonly those whom the mob despises— |  |
|  | "People lacking in judgment, coarse, ill-bred, |  |
|  | "Who know nothing of virtue or its price. |  |
|  | I see, though, that the people mute their envy; |  |
|  | I notice that our court is urged to love me, | 130 |
|  | That peoples subject to my king's dominion |  |
|  | Bow down before me, full of awed respect. |  |
|  | One of the circumcised, a slave, a villain, |  |
|  | Shows me contempt, defies me at all hours. |  |
|  | Neither the rank I hold, nor my own virtue, | 135 |
|  | Nor this royal garment that he sees me dressed in, |  |
|  | Nor this new law which my prince honors me with, |  |
|  | Nor others' example can make him adore me; |  |
|  | Though just one of these should have had the power |  |
|  | To force the haughtiest into humble duty. | 140 |
|  | What! Shall I thus behold my glory slighted, |  |
|  | My credit scorned, my dignity all trampled? |  |
|  | No, no, I want . . . But hush. |  |
| Cyrus: |             You demigods |  |
|  | Ought not to look on these small envious men, |  |
|  | Since their lowly state affords you ample vengeance. | 145 |
|  | "Their hearts, which are consumed by extreme worries, |  |
|  | "Can give to them torments greater by far |  |

| | | |
|---|---|---|
| | "Than what a harsh judge could sentence them to. | |
| Haman: | Indeed? Shall this fine man scorn me unpunished? | |
| | Force me to blush a thousand times a day? | 150 |
| | Shall he wear openly, written on his face, | |
| | What he at least should hide within his thoughts? | |
| Cyrus: | "A lord, I well know, should forestall offenses, | |
| | "As soon as indiscreet souls plan them secretly. | |
| | "If he ignores them, he seems to invite them, | 155 |
| | "And once invited, he can hardly avoid them! | |
| | "For just as one stone taken from its place in | |
| | "A wall will often cause it to fall down, | |
| | "So if some arrogant, reviling man, | |
| | "Urged by malevolence, assaults one's honor, | 160 |
| | "He, using secret stratagems, at last | |
| | "Destroys the edifice, too long neglected. | |
| | "Glory's a ticklish thing and won't stand touching, | |
| | "But just as the eye closes at the approach | |
| | "Of objects that might bring harm to it, so | 165 |
| | "In danger glory should encase itself with prudence, | |
| | "Being like the eyelid, or rather the rampart | |
| | "That can secure it against loss and hazard. | |
| | But to ask again, what man, what boldness does | |
| | Not fear today to be in your disfavor? | 170 |
| | My prince, everyone fears you, and men's honor | |
| | Already designates you for godly rank. | |
| Haman: | Have I not declared that a Jew, accursed race, | |
| | Outrages and despises me at all hours? | |
| Cyrus: | A Jew! Eternal gods! But brazen daring | 175 |
| | Is commonplace among men of that nation. | |
| | "One can change countries, but not one's own nature. | |
| | "When small folk shame the great, there is no insult. | |
| Haman: | I, heretofore so highly ranked by all, | |
| | Could henceforth be a laughingstock, despised? | 180 |
| | May the earth open and hide me in its bowels | |
| | Before such infamy could stain my honor! | |
| | I'd infinitely prefer advancing my death | |
| | Than let someone offend me and not rue it. | |
| Cyrus: | My lord, that is not what I would advise. | 185 |
| Haman: | I'll make the vengeance equal the offense, | |
| | And if possible, exceed it, so that henceforth | |

|  |  |  |
|---|---|---|
| | All men lose the desire ever to hate me. | |
| Cyrus: | Do not get angry for something so minor. | |
| | "Anger is always harmful to the health. | 190 |
| | Without making further outbursts, tell me only | |
| | Against whom you now harbor such resentment. | |
| | If punishment can satisfy your soul, | |
| | This blade will soon drink from his guilty blood, | |
| | So that the whole world may learn by his death | 195 |
| | "That weak men have no right to attack the stronger, | |
| | "But that we must honor those whom the king honors | |
| | "For their rare qualities, and love them, too. | |
| | My lord and master, place reliance in me; | |
| | I've proved my loyalty to you before today. | 200 |
| Haman: | Could my revenge be sated with so little? | |
| | Could just ending his life finish my anger? | |
| | Must not my hand extend still further? I | |
| | Wish this, it is right: let not a single one | |
| | Of the Jews remain alive; let steel and rope | 205 |
| | Be used against them without any mercy; | |
| | No, since I've reached that point, I won't allow | |
| | The unborn children to escape destruction: | |
| | Let them be ripped out of their mothers' wombs, | |
| | And dashed against the walls before their fathers, | 210 |
| | So that they are deprived, along with life, of hope | |
| | To live again through their posterity. | |
| | Let the women be raped in their husbands' sight; | |
| | Let impudent executioners deflower | |
| | Virgins and strangle them next with a noose | 215 |
| | Or throw them downstream, with stones on their necks. | |
| | In short, let smoking blood flow from the throats | |
| | Of the slaughtered Hebrews, sprinkled here and there. | |
| | Let their stinking corpses have no other tombs | |
| | Than hungry dogs and gluttonous birds of prey. | 220 |
| | Let their eternal Lord, great God of Hosts, | |
| | Come to defend them from my active hands! | |
| | Their sighing to heaven is to no avail, | |
| | Nor is their forming sad words, shedding big tears, | |
| | Heaving pitiful cries, making long laments; | 225 |
| | Souls won't be gripped with pity over them. | |
| | Although they reach out with their pleading hands, | |

Imploring mercy from the inhuman swords,
No one will be touched by their woes and spare them.
That's the horrid end that I plan for this people, 230
To quench my fiery anger in their blood:
I want it to be well-known through the world
That Haman has poured out his wrath upon the Jews,
To punish to his taste Mordecai's pride,
And that this vile race, scattered through the earth, 235
Was all one day destroyed for one man's crime.

(*Exeunt.*)

Chorus:
"The sun, as it turns in the sky,
"Cannot see in this lowly place
"An animal that's more abject
"Than the one that's deemed reasonable, 240
"Or one more given to ambition!
    "He promises his vain mind that
"All things must bow beneath his hand,
"That for his sake Phoebus gives light,
"And that all wish to humor him, 245
"So much he delights in being worldly!
    "This man believes the earth is not
"Worthy to hold his footsteps up;
"He thinks that gracious Nature, she
"Who makes him a weak creature, takes 250
"All her delight in him alone.
    "Because he keeps raising himself
"To the summit of slippery honor,
"He thinks he can keep fortune chained,
"That no disgrace can ever come 255
"To dislodge or to cast him down.
    "But hope, which now deceives his heart,
"Will, like an insubstantial vapor,
"Dissolve with him into mere smoke;
"And his so valued reputation 260
"Will be destroyed with his good fortune.
    "Never is royal favor constant:
"Just as it happens in an instant,
"It is withdrawn in a short time.
"More swiftly than a dream, the things 265

"The world admires so much flit by.
 O mushroom sprouted overnight,
You whom pride has so led astray
That, blinded by extremest error,
You cannot truly know yourself, 270
Why do you cause so much ado?
 Do not let your heart be puffed up
With wind that fortune has blown on you,
For though it pushes your ship forward,
Exalting you above great throngs, 275
Your bushel soon shall be filled up.[4]
 "Keep your ambition within bounds
"Appropriate to your condition.
"Is not just one contrary wind
"Or you yourself sufficient to 280
"Destroy you, thwarting your intention?
 "Consider how adversity
"Closely follows prosperity.
"Don't glory so in your good fortune.
"How mad is he who trusts this world! 285
"It is naught but pure vanity.
 "Although all falls out as you wish,
"Fortune may well be treating you
"The way a traitor does, caressing
"While at the same time setting up 290
"An ambush in a secret place.
 "The sweetness of her empty charms
"Quite often leads men to their doom;
"It sets traps to ensnare us, so
"For fear your soul might be deceived, 295
"Stop up your ear and turn away.

## ACT II

*(Enter Ahasuerus.)*

Ahasuerus: To you, immortal gods, I owe immortal
Thanks, for it's you who make my lot so fair
That all past, present and future happiness
Seems to be piled up and stored for me alone.   300
Perhaps your king, that great god of the thunder,
Keeps heaven for himself and gives me earth.
Just as the sun's course is seen over earth's
Whole surface, that's how far my power extends.
"The gods seem to share honors with kings.   305
"Kings come in direct lineage from the gods,
"And, hence, when they are lofty and triumphant,
"They're called on earth the gods' fortunate children,
"A sacred heavenly race that draws its power
"From the supreme force of the eternal essence.   310
"For if one man alone can force obedience
"Upon so many powerful, warlike peoples,
"If a monarch's brow and formidable arm
"And kingly bearing are revered by all,
"If the mere title of emperor or king   315
"Fills brazen hearts with trembling and with fright,
"It's truly your work, powerful Prime Mover,
"Who want our grandeur to resemble yours.
"Therefore, I'm always pleased to iterate
"That God wants to maintain the kings in grandeur   320
"As his lieutenants, giving them an increase
"Of understanding, honor, power and virtue;[5]
"That he's their safeguard and without fail cares
"To act on their behalf when they need help.

"But his greatest favor is without doubt shown 325
"When he causes them to meet a faithful friend
"Who can help ease the heavy, crushing burden
"Imposed on them by wartime and by peacetime,
"Who works ably and hard on state affairs
"And while they sleep keeps watch over their crown, 330
"Who holds the realm securely in his trust
"And by his labors gives them time to rest,
"Who gives good counsel and applies it well,
"Whose aim in all is the honorable and useful;
"In short, whose main concern is not himself, 335
"But who makes public interest come first.
Such a man is Haman, whom you, gracious Heaven,
Produced in our time to give me assistance.
Without his aid I'd hardly have the power
To perform a father's duty toward my subjects. 340
How could I govern six score provinces,
Reconcile great numbers of capricious princes,
Bring hundreds of rich cities 'neath my sway,
If my plans weren't assisted by his arm?
For my royal grandeur I'm renowned as happy, 345
But I deem myself happy to have this man.
The rarest treasures of the orient
Indeed can be no dearer to me than
He. Though I constantly bestow honors on him,
He ought to hope for tributes rarer still: 350
"For doing good to good men as they clearly
"Deserve invites them to still greater effort;
"And, giving honor to a man of honor
"Makes many others strive to emulate him.

*(Enter Haman.)*

But is that not he whom I see approaching? 355
How stern his brow is! He seems rapt in thought.
Fire first would lose its customary heat,
Ice lose its cold, the sun its light, before
He'd be without those plans that cause my fortune
To soar to the zenith that honor can reach. 360
My Haman, here you are; what worthy thought
Keeps you hesitating between diverse options?

II.i.                        HAMAN                        49

Haman:    O formidable prince, O glorious lord,
             Who came down from the skies for all men's welfare,
             I'd be compounded of an ungrateful nature        365
             If, acknowledging myself your humble creature,
             I failed to try at least in some way to
             Respond to the signal honors which you grant me.
             For even though, great king, my feeble power
             Trails far behind what I would like, it seeks        370
             The means to show in all occasions that
             You can't meet a more faithful slave than I;
             Whether you need a watchful eye to uncover
             The plots and stirrings of those troublesome
             Souls who at every turn come to disturb        375
             Your Majesty's rest and destroy your pleasure;
             Or whether, driven by your fiery wrath,
             I lead a mighty army in the field
             Against a mutinous, disloyal people,
             Holding your thunderbolt, like the royal eagle        380
             That brought to Jove the arrows of the tempest
             When that god smashed the heads of the armed Titans
             Upon the fields of Phlegra, where their mad
             Arms tried to scale the high walls of the heavens.
Ahasuerus:    I know that virtue animates your heart        385
             And that your virtue does not idly languish:
             Your helpful counsel and your warlike exploits
             Graft many laurels on our happy olive.
             That's why I honor you myself, my Haman,
             My courtiers praise you and my people worship        390
             You, and if still more honor can be invented,
             I'll always give it to you liberally,
             For what may be excessive in my glory
             Is meant for you alone, so that history notes
             How Ahasuerus did all in his power        395
             To reward your loyal, voluntary service,
             And that, just as his royal grandeur has
             No end, he likewise made your grandeur peerless.
             "A prince never shows limits to his friends,
             "For his favors always go to the extreme.        400
             But you who plan and ponder night and day,
             Using things past to judge of present matters,

          You whose sole care is your king's honor, tell us
          What you were thinking as you came just now.
          For by your facial expression I at once 405
          Knew an important plan was in your mind.
Haman:   You can't but know, my king, with how much zeal
          I aim to raise your august greatness higher;
          And if there's room in my thoughts for another
          Care, may the source of your bounty run dry! 410
          Thus, the many kindnesses you've shown to me
          Have so bound my service and my faith to you
          That I'd feel guilty of a thousand sins,
          If I failed to warn you of a vital matter
          Which may one day cause turmoil in the state. 415
          I merely ask that you lend me your ear.
          There is a people scattered through the earth,
          Useless in peace, unsuitable for war;
          They have their separate laws and differ in
          All things from other nations of the world; 420
          They have no regard for you or your decrees;
          They furnish you no soldiers, pay no taxes;
          Just the reverse; they're flighty and seditious,
          Greedy, disloyal, treacherous, ambitious:
          And, being captives, they feel smoldering rage, 425
          They strive to stir up some civil disturbance
          To shatter your calm, disunite your cities,
          Foment the unleashing of a thousand ills;
          In short, to make a hundred foreign nations,
          Whom you peacefully control, revolt at once. 430
          Sire, it's well known that such beginnings have
          Produced great consequences in the end:
          For just as in the forest a weak spark
          Lies hidden in the ashes of a hollow stump,
          It gradually creeps through the smallest shrubs, 435
          Then burns a thousand ancient trees at once;
          Not one is saved from this loud devastation,
          Which ravages all around with waves of fire,
          Where, had it been put out as it was starting,
          You'd not have seen its fury running through the branches.
          Just so there sometimes comes from a neglected spot 441
          A great uprising that harms everyone.

|            | Besides, when discord starts to blaze in hearts, |     |
|            | It never stops without consuming everything, |     |
|            | Where, if you'd tried early to extinguish it, | 445 |
|            | It wouldn't become widespread and cause alarm. |     |
|            | Then may it please you, great king, promptly to |     |
|            | Command that this vile rabble be attacked, |     |
|            | And that the sword remove from every town |     |
|            | This dissolute race, this accursed people, | 450 |
|            | Devoid of love, of honor, faith and courage. |     |
|            | No act was ever more worthy of a great king. |     |
|            | "If anything distinguishes a ruler, |     |
|            | "It's that he guards good men and ruins the wicked. |     |
|            | My king, then hasten this wished-for result, | 455 |
|            | And to make you still more desirous to |     |
|            | Eradicate this cursed stock, which ought |     |
|            | To find no place in your sweet clemency, |     |
|            | I'm ready to donate ten thousand talents |     |
|            | Of silver; let this race be utterly wiped out!⁶ | 460 |
| Ahasuerus: | But, Haman, still, would it not be unjust |     |
|            | To crush the whole of a peace-loving people? |     |
|            | At least, I've heard no talk of them till now. |     |
| Haman:     | They are a wicked race, innate dissemblers |     |
|            | Who hide their ill will deep within their hearts | 465 |
|            | Until they find occasion to display it. |     |
| Ahasuerus: | "Political unrest is always dangerous; |     |
|            | "Most fortunate is he who can avoid it. |     |
| Haman:     | They are a banished people, without strength or skill, |     |
|            | On whom Heaven pours out its avenging wrath. | 470 |
|            | In truth, they're cowardly but quite malicious, |     |
|            | Disgracing earth and hated by the gods. |     |
|            | Your state will not be jolted by their death; |     |
|            | Nor must you fear that they will use resistance |     |
|            | Against your soldiers whom you urge against them; | 475 |
|            | They have no leader, no support, no money. |     |
|            | Your will alone suffices to defeat them. |     |
|            | But if neglected, they'll cause many problems. |     |
| Ahasuerus: | If things are, Haman, as you represent them, |     |
|            | Let them be wiped out; I give you the power. | 480 |
|            | But make haste, the delay may cause harm. To |     |
|            | "Condemned men any desperate act is possible. |     |

"Their safety lies in not hoping for safety.
Now, so that you can give my men assurance
That this is my will, I give you this seal; 485
Use it as you see fit; I exclude no one.
Also, I'm pleased to issue you the funds
To have this useless race exterminated.

*(Exit.)*

Haman: Then I have reached the goal for which I've waited?
My soul, you go off satisfied and happy. 490
Since by this royal seal I'm authorized
To punish this knave who does not esteem me,
To slay because of him his wretched people
Whom the mere name of Jew makes me judge guilty.
Ha, my sweet braggart, you cannot escape me. 495
I'll make you suffer the most cruel death,
The harshest tortures, the most painful killing
That ever was invented for wrongdoing.
In vain you'll rue the error of your pride,
With anguish in your heart, tears in your eyes. 500
Your wretched end will put a stop to envy,
The shadow currently clouding my greatness.
You've too greatly defied, despised and flouted
Me to be favored with a pardon now.
I want you, without hope of mercy or delay, 505
To taste the sweet fruit brought forth by your boldness.
This time we'll see whether this thrice great God
Can rescue you from my avenging arms.
It's said he made you pass through the Red Sea
And drowned the Egyptians entering its depths; 510
It's said that he led you through empty deserts,
By day with the cloud wandering through the air,
By night with the flame shining in the darkness;
That he for forty years clothed your host, fed them
In barren lands with manna from the heavens; 515
That he delayed for you the setting of the sun,
Knocked down the walls of a city under siege,
Defeated thirty kings who warred against you,
Subdued with his hand heaps of people for you
And split the waters of the Jordan River;[7] 520

To sum up, he performed more miracles for you
Than credulous ears ever will believe.
And yet his hand, too weak for my designs,
Won't manage to free you from my hands today.
No, I don't have a heart so softened by fear      525
That your old wives' tales could make any impression.
Come on, invisible, unknown and lying God,
Show how you want to be judged in the future.
Your arm must not be idle at this moment;
By this one act reveal whether you've any power.  530
Haman shall openly take arms against you:
He has on his side the king's authority,
Experienced soldiers from a hundred vast
Lands, popular support and princes' favor,
Silver and gold, great might and courage. Can     535
He with all that not be victorious?
Although they boast you are unconquerable,
In spite of you I'll ruin your wretched people,
Wretched indeed and foolish utterly,
To rely for aid on what they do not see,          540
On a God who always has allowed a hundred
Diverse peoples to defeat them. What fine glory!
Be it known henceforth to posterity
That, angered in both word and deed by Haman,
This God of Israel took no vengeance on him;      545
That his wrath is a sham, his power likewise;
That he's a nameless God, an ineffectual dream;
That he's no creator; naught can come from naught!
That he does not determine battles' outcome,
But was invented to deceive this rabble,[8]       550
Who are the dregs and sewer of the universe.[9]
"There's no limit, no end to superstition,
"And it has no feature commoner than error.
But let's stop speaking and begin to act.
"By lengthy speeches time is often lost           555
"That would be better used to get results,
"And anger is used up by too much speaking.
I'm off to see my man quickly dispatched.[10]

(*Exit.*)

Chorus: "The anger of offended princes
"Is a thing greatly to be feared,
"For it keeps burning and is never
"Extinguished in their furious hearts.
    "Their soul, when once it's set ablaze
"By this brisk and devouring fire,
"Becomes filled with so much black smoke
"That it's blinded in other matters.
    "Just as, in a dark, heavy fog
"Small bodies may appear as large,
"However small the insult is,
"The force of anger makes it grow.
    "Those who commit the least offense
"Receive the harshest punishment.
"Vengeance is utterly excessive
"When it is carried out in anger.
    "Remove that speck that is extended
"Over the eye of your understanding,
"And the daylight shall be restored
"Unto its blinded power of judgment.[11]
    "When one's power of imagination
"Is once filled with a false impression,
"It is immediately seized
"With that fiery emotion, anger.
    "The person who's afraid of shame
"Comes to be fearful at all hours
"That he does not receive as much
"Esteem as he thinks he deserves.
    "Through this misjudgment he requests
"A thing that cannot be his due,
"Namely, the honor which great God
"Commands to be paid to him alone.
    "Is this not the extreme of error,
"To dare presume to such excess?
"No one who truly knows himself
"Will make himself be so esteemed.
    "No creature ever has been seen
"Taking the place of the Creator
"Without having to face a sudden
"Descent to misery for this madness.

"It thus is too presumptuous
"For man, a fragile, mortal being, 600
To think himself in his conceit
Deserving of religious worship.
    You peacock, if your feathers make
You proud, to see so many lovely
Mirrors, at least cast down your eyes 605
Upon your black and dirty feet.

# ACT III

(*Enter Mordecai.*)

Mordecai:  If I had to be born in such an adverse
　　　　　Time, to be welcomed by a swarm of ills,
　　　　　I wish my eyes had been covered by darkness
　　　　　The moment they were opened to the light!　　　610
　　　　　Ah, why was not my cradle my tomb, also?[12]
　　　　　O stunted, wretched man, abhorred by nature!
　　　　　Would I could shed as many tears today
　　　　　As I feel sorrows teeming in my heart!
　　　　　Would I could form as many just laments　　　615
　　　　　As I receive cruel blows within my soul!
　　　　　Would I could heave as many bitter moans
　　　　　As storms are locked up in my troubled mind!
　　　　　I'd have to change my eyes into two fountains,
　　　　　To use a thousand voices to relate　　　620
　　　　　My pain, and night and day borrow the winds;
　　　　　"But maybe ills, lamented, are too light to bear.
　　　　　O Lord, I well know that heaps of offenses
　　　　　Call down on us your vengeance, much delayed;
　　　　　That our transgressions of your sacred law　　　625
　　　　　Change you from gentle father to awesome judge,
　　　　　That our ostentatious pride and haughty boldness
　　　　　Dry up the springs of your grace over Israel;
　　　　　In short, that you see only with a wrathful eye
　　　　　The Hebrew remnants, scattered far and wide.　　　630
　　　　　You reduced them to the chains of foreign nations,
　　　　　In order, by their hands, to avenge your honor,
　　　　　Betrayed so basely by this insolent people,
　　　　　Who live under a harsh, distressing yoke.

Should I not rather say they'll cease to live? 635
Do you want to pursue them to the edge of
The grave, driven from place to place, just as
Whirlwinds sweep straws from field to field?
If you are pleased to weigh the horror of
Our vice upon the scales of your holy justice, 640
We never must expect a pardon. Death
"Alone remains as punishment for sin.
The sea has fewer waves in a storm's fury,
And fewer hairs abound upon our heads
Than our heart and our hands produce of sins. 645
It's just the face that makes us look like humans.
But if our recourse is to your compassion,
May it henceforth grant mercy to repentance;
May it champion our cause and lend us aid
Against the curst scheme of this fiendish tiger 650
Set to devour us; may it offer you,
To bend your wrath, the tears of a sighing folk
Who raise their hands and hearts upward to heaven,
To lessen the blow struck by your just rigor.
Your sacred majesty was long ago offended 655
By our ancestors, both in deed and thought;
A hundred times you exposed them to the wishes
Which their enemies made to do them harm.
When finally they came to weep for their offense,
At once you took them back in your protective care; 660
So greatly does your goodness overcome sins
When men are angered to have angered you!
Lord, in our lifetime make us recognize again
That you don't disown the people who adore you:
For though they have unworthily defiled 665
Themselves with all foul sins, you yourself chose them;
Yourself selected them to get the birthright,
Although aware of what their hearts would be.
For this unique honor you released their necks
From Egypt's chains after a preset time, 670
Led them dry-shod across a sea and drowned
The unbelieving and rebellious army
Of their pursuing foes, who made so bold
To try out paths forbidden to their feet.

But, O great God of miracles, I don't want to 675
Start on the peerless works of your peerless hands,
Seeing that I'd try in vain to tell them all,
Had I a tongue of bronze, a mouth of iron.
All this wide universe fights in your service,
Lies within the great scope of your high justice: 680
Nothing is done or said except by your
Will, and all that you want is carried out at once.
Thus it was your voice that made earth and heaven:
The great and rare things which these both contain
Show stamped on their surface the marks of your fingers:
The animals, both of the fields and forests, 686
The nomadic troupes spread through the empty air,
The scaly tribes that play throughout the waters,
And lastly, all there ever was or must be of
Humans received their being from your hands. 690
Not only did you make this round machine:
But having built so fair a world from chaos,
As absolute master, all-embracing, self-contained,
You came to impose a law on every being
Which, keeping them ever unchangeable, 695
Preserves nature and makes her last forever:
For though all things fall back into that vast sea, they
Meet again in it and quickly take new forms.
Besides, you alone know the most hidden things.
No souls were ever closed to your eyes. Their 700
Rays pierce our hearts, just as the sun goes through
A stained glass window, exposed to its eye.
If, therefore, I have not revered this bully,
Whose insolent pride's directed against you;
If I have not bowed head or knees to him 705
To flatter his heart that's incensed against us,
You know if it was done presumptuously.
"To holy magistrates one owes respect,
And I'm not so deceived by self-love that
I scorned him just to overprize myself. 710
But then, kind sun, may you stop shining on me
When I'm seen to displease immortal God
In order to please man, or if, base deserter,
I put a creature in the Creator's place.

III.i. HAMAN

|  | I know how God's heart burns with jealousy | 715 |
|---|---|---|
|  | When man, guiding himself by his caprices, |  |
|  | Wants to make men divine and worship them. |  |
|  | "Far better to die than revere a false god. |  |
|  | You, therefore, true God, God of clemency, |  |
|  | Erase our sins and leniently remember | 720 |
|  | Your suffering people who direct their faith to |  |
|  | You, not for love of them, but for love of you. |  |
|  | Drive from their minds so many gloomy fears, |  |
|  | Rekindle their light, make their darkness shine, |  |
|  | Transform their tears to joy, their griefs to pleasure, | 725 |
|  | And shower on Haman the calamities |  |
|  | That seem to be aimed at our guiltless heads. |  |
|  | But if your hand shields us, such storms are vain. |  |
|  | Among us only your name is invoked. |  |
|  | Will you allow man to destroy its fame? | 730 |
|  | Will you stop the mouths of the people who praise you, |  |
|  | Who own you as Savior and name you Creator?[13] |  |
|  | Will those who are enclosed in dusty tombs |  |
|  | Rise up again from death's dark bosom |  |
|  | In order to proclaim among the heathens | 735 |
|  | The deathless honors of your holy praises?[14] |  |
|  | Make haste, therefore, O God; please rescue us |  |
|  | From the roaring lion who's poised to devour us; |  |
|  | Fasten his gaping jaws and check his fury. |  |
|  | Eternal Shepherd, oh defend your flock. | 740 |

*(Exit; enter Sarah and Rachel.)*

Sarah: Can I recognize him in this garb? Is this[15]
Then Mordecai? God, what a change! Do you
See him, dear sister, all deformed with filth,
Beating his chest, his face all pale and dry,
As he breathes sighs and dissolves into tears? 745
Such grief comes only from supreme misfortunes.
Rachel: O strange and woeful sight! But here's the queen.
Let's quickly tell her of his unbelievable
Sorrow.

*(Enter Esther.)*

Esther: Tell me, I pray, what violent
Grief makes these tears now fall from your eyes? What

|  |  |  |
|---|---|---|
|  | Cloud, spread over your lovely faces, changes | 751 |
|  | The customary grace of their sweet look? |  |
| Rachel: | Our eyes have just beheld a piteous sight: |  |
|  | Mordecai, in a sad, disastrous state, |  |
|  | Is shedding copious tears from his moist eyes; | 755 |
|  | He burdens Heaven with wishes, fills it with |  |
|  | Prayers, having covered his gray head with dust, |  |
|  | Having totally bared his panting chest, |  |
|  | And placed a stinging hair-shirt on his back. |  |
|  | O God, how he has changed his normal manner! | 760 |
|  | One would have taken him, viewed carefully, |  |
|  | For a speaking dead man just out of his grave. |  |
| Esther: | My uncle, my support, what mortification |  |
|  | Can thus have befallen you today? What ill |  |
|  | Is so severe, what torment so cruel that | 765 |
|  | They can disturb your blissful spirit to this point? |  |
|  | Is it ambition, that makes life a torture? |  |
|  | The biting thirst for gold, or cursed envy? |  |
|  | No, your heart won't admit passions so base; |  |
|  | God only has found room in your affections. | 770 |
|  | What is the matter then? Go, sweet companions, |  |
|  | Go tell him from me: Esther knows that you |  |
|  | Bathe your eyes in big tears and beat your breast |  |
|  | And tear at your face with a cruel hand. |  |
|  | But she can't understand (that's why she sends us) | 775 |
|  | What storm is interfering with the calm of |  |
|  | Your joy. Take clothing from my private room |  |
|  | To dress him in after he has washed. Go, |  |
|  | Quickly attend to what I am commanding, |  |
|  | For meanwhile I remain in great distress. | 780 |

*(Exeunt Sarah and Rachel.)*

"Indeed, one does not shed the feeling of
"Ills when one puts on royal finery.
"With its pomp, majesty is just as quick
"To sadness as the despised and lowly people.
"For each few flowers, it has a thousand thistles; 785
"Next to its pleasures, sorrows bud, just as
"The rose is seen to bloom next to the thorn.
"How rare a thing to live with no pain! Yet

"That is not all; our own emotions turn
"Bitterly harsh through the afflictions which         790
"Our friends endure; for royal grandeur does
"Not blot out loyal friendships from the heart.
Behold that good old man, that uncle to whom I
Owe, after God, all the honor which the king
Gave me, who gives way to despondency.               795
The firm bond of love which links our spirits makes
Me a participant in his sad languor;
The blow of his distress reaches my heart.
But whence comes this pain in his dejected soul?
Does he feel some regret to see me raised            800
To the supreme degree of lofty honor,
Which to mad humans seems the utmost happiness?
Does he not fear I'll sin, seeing me seated
Amid a people who're not circumcised?
Or rather (may kind Heaven avert this mishap)        805
That this royal diadem around my heart will
Make me forget God? Cease, my second father,
To fear for me this favorable grandeur;
I would deem my good fortune unhappiness,
If God, our great God, had not so ordained,          810
To show in our days that his great bounty makes
A sea of riches overflow in lowly places.
If royal rank prevented me from serving
Him who gives riches and can take them back,
I'd rather grovel with the common people             815
Than reign in glory on Ahasuerus' throne.
I know the difference between this world's mire
And Heaven's riches, which we must esteem.
This paltry opulence and this vain pomp
With dazzling lustre may deceive some other          820
Fool; they won't blind my youthful understanding,
For I make use of them solely to serve God.
Neither the sweet words of the king, my husband,
Nor the blunt, ribald humor of his jesters, nor
My stately garments, fringed with gold and silver,   825
Nor the long row of people in my retinue,
Nor the dainty foods with which my table's laden,
Nor the proud palace where I see I'm lodged

        Lead my heart astray after the vanities
        Which I see worldly folk swept away by madly.    830
        My taste, blunted by such insipid pleasures,
        Makes me seek sweeter occupation elsewhere.[16]
        Lord, you grant me that, reflecting on your law,
        I nurture night and day my sprouting faith.
        The sacred reading of your just commandments    835
        Renews in my soul fear and love for you;
        And your divine laws serve me as a torch
        That in the night of death will guide my steps.

        (*Reenter Sarah and Rachel.*)

        But see, my faithful servant girls are back;
        I go to meet them. What? Their moist eyes make    840
        Once more a river swelling high with tears.
        For what purpose, O God, is this new grief?
        Then do you wish our doom? O gracious Lord,
        Do not in your harsh anger punish us.

**Sarah:**    We did your bidding, but in vain, however.    845
        I also had brought this rich garment to
        Clothe your uncle in, but he refused to take it.
        He did not deign to give one word of answer.
        I fear that he may try to take his life;
        He weeps incessantly, always laments;    850
        The wound of his sharp grief is very deep;
        But, this is the worst part, he won't have it probed.
        "A patient's case is dire when he won't care
        "To apply the needed treatment for his sickness.

**Esther:**    O Lord almighty! What possesses him?    855
        To hide his problem thus, to shun the cure!
        Ah, can he, I ask you, indulge his sorrow,
        To keep it hidden from his faithful Esther?
        Might he have wrongly taken offense at me,
        Or thought my voice could contradict my feelings?    860
        Has he known me to be such? Wretched old man,
        Were I presented with a hundred tortures,
        To turn away the love so strong and constant
        Which you wrongly doubt—error transports you so—
        Yet I'd gladly value tortures less than nothing,    865
        Provided that even in death you pleased to love me.

III.i.

*(She signals to Hatach.)*

Go then, my dear Hatach, my faithful servant,
To find out the torment which that cruel man hides from me.

Hatach: I hurry, to remove the sorrow from
Your heart, doubt from your mind, tears from your eyes. 870

*(Exeunt; enter Mordecai with Chorus of Jews.)*

Chorus: Eternal God, don't make your vengeance fall
Upon your captive folk seized with repentance;
You always were so merciful, so gentle,
Do not make them breathe in your anger's gall.
Put back your sword of justice in its sheath, 875
For if all have erred, they all confess their sin.[17]

Mordecai: Holy people of Zion, let's turn back to God
And sing this hymn to him in our affliction.

    The heathen, having entered your holy portion,
Have profaned our temple and pillaged its treasures; 880
The great Jerusalem, exposed to havoc,
Saw its fortresses turned into heaps of stone.

    Your people's flesh was given to the birds
Of prey who prowl about the skies for food;
The gluttonous appetites of bears and wolves 885
Made tasty meals out of the sons of Isaac.

    They had their blood poured out like running water;
It filled to overflowing all the crossroads;
No one has buried their ill-smelling corpses;
Their horrid skeletons lie in the fields half-eaten. 890

    Jacob serves as a byword to the gentiles,
The shameful plaything of the nearby peoples;
They all hurl many mocking words at him,
As if they found contentment in his woes.

    How long, O God? Inside your soul shall spite 895
For seeing yourself offended seethe forever?
Shall the flame of your wrath be forever blazing?
Shall your heart forever be throbbing with fury?

    Rather come pour the vessels of your anger
Upon the nations which reject your power, 900
Which don't deign even to hear your great name;
And make us now perceive your saving grace.

    They nearly have devoured the race of Jacob,

They nearly have devoured the race of Jacob,
And their hands dared to raze to the foundations
The marvelous city walls of your rich Zion, 905
Which the fire, more merciful, refused to burn.
   Remember not our faults of former times;
Inform us speedily of your compassion;
Or else the sorrows which accumulate in
Our hearts will make us sink under crushing torments. 910
   God of our salvation, for the love of your
Glory, firmly support the circumcised race
And guard, by guarding us, the memory of your name,
Which by our death alone they wish to kill.
   Why shall the people with profane lips say: 915
What happened to the God they used to call on?
Be touched at last by dear care of your servants,
And don't permit them to mock you through us.
   From orient until the ends of earth
May the wicked be known by their punishment, 920
In order that henceforth none shall wage war
Against the God of Gods, seated in Zion.
   May the humble moaning of so many slaves
Arrive at your ear, good and mighty God,
And use your power to keep us all alive 925
While our foes are condemning us to death.
   Render to Haman, who, afire with anger,
Has openly sworn to massacre your people,
Twice seven times the shameful degradation
Which he's procured to you, more than to us. 930
   Then shall the holy flock of your holy pasture
Perpetually bless your aid, and greatly
Moved by wonderment and reverence, they shall
Recount your glory to posterity.[18]

*(Enter Hatach.)*

Hatach:   The queen has sent me to you, good old man, 935
        To learn what subject makes you suffer so.
        What? Once again I see your tears redouble?
        "A constant heart ought not to get upset.
        But finally, I beg, don't hide the cause
        That puts a stinging hairshirt on your shoulder; 940

III.i.  HAMAN

   Indeed, this crude garment is unsuitable
   To you, a near relation of the queen.
Mordecai: If I've some reason to moan and lament
   The fortune of my people, which fate wants
   To bind up with my own, Hatach, you'll learn it,   945
   And maybe you'll weep with me for our woes.
   Haman, enraged to see the Jewish people
   Living tranquilly under a peaceful king,
   Who in the happy shade spread by his laurels
   Makes fertile olive-trees resprout and flourish;   950
   With no reason, no subject, plots in secret
   To expunge our memory and destroy us all,
   Falsely accusing us of trumped-up crimes;
   He offers silver to pay lavishly
   The barbarous executioners, who wish   955
   With cruel hand to exterminate this faithful
   Race, who deserve, O Heaven, the opposite of death,
   If holy justice dwelt down here on earth.
   But the decree is given, the dispatches
   Sent out. So weep now, Mordecai, and sigh,   960
   You wretched old man, destined by Heaven to
   See holy Jacob wiped out in one blow;
   To see fierce soldiers with their bloody swords
   Drive out the trembling soul from old men's chests;
   To see virgins in vain clasping the knees   965
   Of butchers blinded by barbaric anger;
   To see small babies at their mothers' breast
   Turn a white sword-blade crimson with their blood;
   In short, to see a thousand horrors with these very
   Eyes, then receive a wild sword in my heart.   970
   Would that Heaven's wrath, which vents itself on us,
   Permitted me to die in armed attack,
   When I still had the heart and function to
   Defend our walls, a cutlass in my hand!
   Would that I'd lost my life in that horrid bloodshed   975
   Where I saw Persians act dementedly,[19]
   Where I saw the entirety of the holy city
   Become rich booty for the angry Mede!
   Where I saw the altars used for sacrifices
   Basely profaned with filth and unclean things!   980

Thrice happy are you, wretched citizens,
Who then endured a painful death in view
Of your relations; O great-hearted race,
I call you thrice and even four times happy,
Not for your having died amidst the fighting, 985
But for not living now through so much killing.
Thus, if, my dear Hatach, you wish to help
In the abject plight that you see us reduced to,
Return to Esther and tell her from me
That her country is today in utmost danger. 990
Let her therefore go to the king and plead
That proud Haman not touch her innocent people,
That she prevent the enforcement of the edict,
Which this inhuman heart wishes and aims for.

(*Exit Hatach.*)

Strengthen her feeble heart, O kindly God, 995
Against all the violence of this cruel storm;
Forge so many pleasing glances in her eyes,
So many smiles on her mouth and such charming
Smiles; make from her tongue's sweetness so much honey
And mix such force in the words of her oration 1000
That her glances and charms, her words and smiles
Might pierce and burn and charm the spirits of
King Ahasuerus, so that by his mercy
We may avoid the death this villain plans for us.
O God, make it redound on his own head. 1005
Perhaps it pleases you once more, O Almighty,
To operate through a weak woman's arm,
To save your Isaac from death and dishonor.
"Although your arsenal is fully furnished
"With many horrid plagues with which the world is 1010
"Punished; although heaven, fire, air, sea and earth
"For you march off to war under your standard,
"Yet several times you made our rescue spring
"From an apparent nothing when it pleased you;
"In order that, indeed, in human weakness 1015
"Your sovereign strength might show forth all the better.
What even a thousand famous warriors failed to
Achieve, though they could count numerous laurels

|                                                                                      |      |
|--------------------------------------------------------------------------------------|------|
| Within a bulwark, in the heart of battle,                                            | 1020 |
| So many Sauls and strong Jonathans; this,                                            |      |
| I say, was done by a shepherd boy of twenty.[20]                                     |      |
| "For this and scores of similar works all call you                                   |      |
| "The marvel of the gods and God of marvels,                                          |      |
| "You who make the strong man weak, the weak man strong,                              |      |
| "Who make the living die, revive the dead,                                           | 1026 |
| "Who at last deliver from enemy hands                                                |      |
| "Those for whose rescue hope itself despairs;                                        |      |
| "You only have the power to change our fate,                                         |      |
| "And as you please, you lead it to your ends.                                        | 1030 |
| Let's draw faith from our ancient history.                                           |      |
| You, Egypt's terror and Israel's glory,                                              |      |
| Moses, great prophet and great Hebrew leader,                                        |      |
| Did you not once go wandering all over,                                              |      |
| A straying nomad from a nomadic people,                                              | 1035 |
| To avoid the chains put on your captive race;                                        |      |
| When at the burning bush God appeared to you?[21]                                    |      |
| His awesome voice told you: Go to the king                                           |      |
| Whose throne I plant on the Egyptian shore;                                          |      |
| Command him to remove your people's bondage                                          | 1040 |
| In the name of the thrice-Great who, seated in                                       |      |
| Heaven, moderates the universe with one blink.                                       |      |
| He'll place numerous obstacles in your way,                                          |      |
| But you'll oppose his efforts with your miracles.                                    |      |
| Thus it pleased you to choose this great law-giver,                                  | 1045 |
| Who through the deserts served to guide the children                                 |      |
| Of Abraham, who then had hope of neither                                             |      |
| A liberator nor deliverance,                                                         |      |
| And the Egyptians suspected even less that                                           |      |
| From there would come their doom and the Hebrews' safety.                            |      |
| "No one has total knowledge of your secrets;                                         | 1051 |
| "In too bright lights the human eye sees nothing.                                    |      |

*(Reenter Hatach.)*

|         |                                                                          |      |
|---------|--------------------------------------------------------------------------|------|
|         | But don't I see Hatach returning toward me?                              |      |
|         | May he at least give me some comfort by                                  |      |
|         | Reporting to me that Esther's resolved                                   | 1055 |
|         | To plead with the king for her unloved people.                           |      |
| Hatach: | I've not forgotten anything you ordered;                                 |      |

| | | |
|---|---|---|
| Hatach: | I've not forgotten anything you ordered; | |
| | The queen knows why you mourn, she adds her tears, | |
| | She adds her sighing; and her humble prayers | |
| | Speak unto God from her eyelids and heart. | 1060 |
| | But for her to go now find his majesty, | |
| | She bitterly regrets, there is no means; | |
| | The more so, you recall, since an express command | |
| | Currently forbids the royal presence to her. | |
| | But without infringement of her duty's laws, | 1065 |
| | The point when she can see him is quite near; | |
| | She soon expects to be called back by him. | |
| Mordecai: | Is she so zealous for her people, then? | |
| | Can such a weak consideration stop her? | |
| | "Not even death ought to delay good acts. | 1070 |
| | "O God, how harmful is prosperous greatness! | |
| | Return to whence you came, tell her that she | |
| | Shouldn't hope to save herself on that sad day; | |
| | The shipwreck covers all; she can't escape; | |
| | That if our hope's forsaken by her, we | 1075 |
| | May be given deliverance from elsewhere, | |
| | But she and her house, through her lack of courage, | |
| | Will feel the rigor of the eternal hand. | |
| | Does she not see that she was raised to this rank | |
| | To calm the storm stirred up unexpectedly? | 1080 |
| | To get her people out of this mortal danger | |
| | Into which a foreign slave's pride casts them? God | |
| | "Disposes of all things, God foresees all. | |
| | Go, propose to her what I propose to you.[22] | |

(*Exeunt.*)

| | | |
|---|---|---|
| Chorus: | "Whene'er affliction weighs on you, | 1085 |
| | "Address your prayer to the Lord; | |
| | "Without fear come present yourself. | |
| | "Naught pleases him more than to listen | |
| | "To men who call upon his goodness | |
| | "With eyes, with mouth and with the soul. | 1090 |
| | "Even when heaven, sea and land | |
| | "Already have declared war on you, | |
| | "And you are viewed as surely doomed, | |
| | "The only person on your side, | |

"Implore the everlasting grace; 1095
"It surely will take up your quarrel.
   "The powers that were assailing you
"Will undertake then to defend you;
"Heaven, as well as land and sea,
"Will quickly take arms in your aid; 1100
"Grasping his thunderbolt, God himself
"Will smash your enemies to dust.
   "But if he wants to put you to
"The test, make sure he finds you full
"Of courage; don't fear to shed blood, 1105
"To remain steadfast at your post:
"He who fights and wins victory
"Deserves great glory as his prize.
   "The warrior who is fazed by blows
"Never gains victor's palms or crowns. 1110
"It is the outcome of the combat
"That makes the soldier's mettle known;
"Only the peril of a skirmish
"Shows how his courage should be judged.
   "The man who with a cowardly 1115
"Heart fears the squalls of a great storm
"Should not commit himself to the sea.
"But he must not be terrified
"To see his ship tossed to and fro
"And threatened by the waves and winds. 1120
   "Let no one join the holy troupe
"If he is frightened of afflictions.
"They always face many a danger;
"Yet the ship of the faithful church
"Is never seen to sink or founder, 1125
"As it sails in a cruel sea.
   "The cross unceasingly is fastened
"Upon the wholly bruised, chafed shoulder
"Of those whom God most cherishes;
"Nevertheless, cheerful and joyous, 1130
"They walk upon the painful path
"That leads to the celestial city.[23]
   "Once they arrive, the choir of angels
"Intones their praises before God;

"And God himself, stirred by their love, 1135
"Burns them with his love night and day,
"And as he mingles with their souls,
"Ravishes them with pleasant flames.
   O saintly and most blessed race,
Live then forever in his grace; 1140
And when you're freed from mortal combat,
Relax on that eternal Sabbath,
The glorious day of which shall never
Come to an end or cease to be.

# ACT IV

*(Enter Esther, Sarah and Rachel.)*

Esther: Though I should die there, I'll incur the danger.  1145
To leave my people prey to a stranger's pride,
To view their ruin unmixed while I am sheltered,
To rejoice, while I'm in port, to see them shipwrecked?
May my heart cease to beat, my limbs to move
When I'd even conceive a plan so base!  1150
I certainly prefer to share their fortune
Than to drag out an unwelcome life thereafter.
"It's pleasing to die with our dear friends, if
"Living with them no longer is permitted.
Come, Esther, you must suffer in their suffering,  1155
Or else deliver them in your deliverance.
I ask, what use is this crown on my head
If I'm too weak to avert this great disaster?
What use this royal sceptre which adorns my hand
If I've no power, no credit with my master?  1160
What must be left for me, except to die well,
If I cannot rescue my race from death?
He who in his hands holds the destinies of life
Will not permit it; he's urged by his glory;
Or if he does permit it, I've this comfort,  1165
That I will die for him. But I'm quite wrong,
For if he shuts my eyes to earthly darkness,
It's to reopen them to eternal light.
Still, if the king loves me, he won't allow
Me to be dragged to death, I being blameless,  1170
And out of love for me, his dearest wife,
He'll save all my race. You give me that hope,

You who at your wish bend the hearts of kings;
Then grant me the result as well as the hope. (*to Sarah*.)
Come lend your shoulder; I must lean on it; 1175
Pain weakens me. (*to Rachel*.) I beg you, walk ahead.

(*Esther moves from her apartments toward the royal
throne room accompanied by Sarah and Rachel. Ahasuerus
watches her, accompanied by Haman and Arphaxat.*)

Ahasuerus: What paradise of love my eyes now glimpse!
It leads my sight astray, makes my mind wander.
Is that my lovely Esther I perceive?
I think I know her by her noble bearing. 1180
See how she makes her solemn steps flow smoothly.
Juno herself would not equal her walk.
But here she is quite close. I must pretend a little.
Let her, as well as love me, learn to fear me.
"By fear we make this sex return to duty. 1185
She comes without summons; that is not permitted.

Esther: Girls, hold me up, support me. I am fainting.

Ahasuerus: What's wrong, my soul, my dear love, my most precious?
If you collapse, at least fall in my arms.
This slight misdeed of yours will not be punished. 1190
The edict is made for the common people.
Esther, come to, regain your normal color.
This sceptre's placed on you as sign of pardon.
O queen of my heart, give your king a kiss.

Esther: My soul, as if thunderstruck at seeing you, 1195
Felt that fault, O king whose august majesty
Is sacred for me and will always be,
As long as my life's thread shall last.
I thought you were an angel wrapped in glory.
The splendor of your face forced me to think so, 1200
And this fire blazing out from atop your head . . .
But alas! support me, I again am fainting.[24]

Ahasuerus: Why, what is wrong, my Esther, my dear, sweet
Life? Why have you so soon taken from me
This light which alone can bring day to my spirit? 1205
Why do you hide yourselves, fair suns of love,
Who in my soul with contrary effect
Produce sometimes cold icicles, sometimes flame?

|  |  |  |
|---|---|---|
|  | If you're still conscious, look upon your spouse; |  |
|  | Do it, if not from love, at least from pity. | 1210 |
|  | How cold she is! O grief! How I'm distressed! |  |
| Arphaxat:[25] | No, sire, it's nothing but a sudden fright |  |
|  | Which, passing lightly like a flash of lightning, |  |
|  | Prevents the normal movement of her spirits. |  |
|  | See, she comes to. | 1215 |
| Ahasuerus: | Ah wretched prince! If it |  |
|  | Should chance that she whom you find most attractive, |  |
|  | Because of your austere look, suffers death, |  |
|  | Then die with boldness and do not survive her. |  |
| Arphaxat: | Rejoice, sire; see, she's getting up. |  |
| Ahasuerus: | Esther, you're like the flower, greatly battered | 1220 |
|  | By a cruel storm, which later has its vigor |  |
|  | Revived as the sun casts its rays upon it. |  |
|  | Fair soul, to whom I owe the pleasures of my life, |  |
|  | Say with no more delay what you desire. |  |
|  | "I want to make it yours; she who possesses | 1225 |
|  | "The king can dispose of all; I'm no more my |  |
|  | Own. Then ask without fear; the words you utter |  |
|  | Will be at once rewarded with fulfilment. |  |
| Esther: | O prince, whom glory must raise to the stars, |  |
|  | Since it has pleased you to cast down your eyes on me, | 1230 |
|  | Granting still more by your distinguished mercy |  |
|  | Than I had ever promised to my humble |  |
|  | Heart, may it please your majesty to attend |  |
|  | The banquet I've prepared for you alone just now; |  |
|  | Yet, if you please, let Haman also join us. | 1235 |
|  | And that alone, great king, I ask you now. |  |
| Ahasuerus: | My Esther, is that all? It's not much, truly. |  |
|  | Haman, since she wishes, let's go there at once. |  |

(*Exeunt.*)

|  |  |  |
|---|---|---|
| Chorus: | "Expect deliverance from heaven; |  |
|  | "Hope for salvation from the Lord. | 1240 |
|  | "From that place all good things arise; |  |
|  | "And fear of him provides assurance |  |
|  | "To hearts that naturally are |  |
|  | "Meek, to offset the fears of death. |  |
|  | "Sometimes to punish the outrageous | 1245 |

"Conduct of those ambitious persons
"Who spew forth insults against heaven,
"He makes a woman's courage grow
"To such extent that she dares try
"Feats that might terrify a man. 1250
   "Audacity amid the risks
"That roll across the field of battle
"Is without doubt a gift of God's
"Grace, not a natural recklessness
"That makes the most extreme of dangers 1255
"Appear rather as light and small.
   "A thousand times this soldier has
"Been seen to fight without being worried;
"The enemies' redoubled efforts
"Have been unable to destroy him; 1260
"He, totally surprised and stunned,
"Now acts the coward and runs away.
   "This timid man, on the other hand,
"Whose very shadow frightened him,
"Feels his heart armed with fortitude 1265
"When God wants to make him courageous,
"In such a way that he'd not fear
"The horror of ten thousand deaths.
   "Therefore, to demonstrate his power
"And make it known to humans that 1270
"Against the blows which his hands deal
"Resistance has less force than glass,
"He effortlessly will confound
"The stronger by the weaker man.
   "It is so that the greatness of 1275
"His judgments may appear more clearly
"And so that by their outcome we
"Can recognize his providence.
"The eye that cannot read this picture
"Is covered up by a black blindfold! 1280
   "Simply because your heart is lofty,
Because you hold the foremost rank,
Commander of so many warriors,
Don't overestimate your strength.
"If God so wills, this force avails, 1285

"And can do naught, if God's unwilling.
   Then boast less of your strength and pride,
Or else you'll see them beaten down;
Don't be swept away through too much daring
And set limits to your desire.   1290
"For he who does not know his measure
"Is wholly ruined in the end.

# ACT V

*(Enter Haman and Zeresh.)*

Haman: Ever since the Sun kindled its torch to spread
Daylight anew upon the world, by tracing
An oblique path through the Zodiac, where   1295
Without end he redoes his daily course,
Of all the mortals none can with good reason
Compete with me for the comparison.
Many men are known who, living far from war,
Have tilled the land with a hundred yokes of oxen,   1300
Have made countless fat flocks cover the fields
Where it seemed snow was gleaming on their skins.
But these rich peasants, living without glory,
Died likewise without leaving a memorial;
And the same grave which received their bones enclosed 1305
Their fame, devoid of honor and of praise.
Many others have come, who by countless exploits,
The praise of which equalled the gods in glory,
Attained world fame and gained renown from honor,
Who lacked in death, however, the good fortune   1310
To live again in a continuous line
Through their sons and make their race known to all ages.
But I, who keep Fortune locked up in my hand,
Amass today all the human good fortune
That's scattered variously on all these people,   1315
And I still surpass them in advantages.
I've wealth, estates, renown, influence and
Many fine sons who will inherit my
Name, wealth and glory, and, I further hope,
Carry on the virtues by whose luster I   1320

|  |  |  |
|---|---|---|
|  | Am honored. Yet all this will not content me, | |
|  | So long as Mordecai sits at the door. | |
|  | My eyes won't get an instant's quiet sleep | |
|  | Until I am avenged upon that wretch. | |
|  | Did I not meet him as I left the palace? | 1325 |
|  | Far from displaying more humility | |
|  | For the approaching peril threatening his life, | |
|  | A visible spite was painted on his face, | |
|  | And as with sunken eyes he watched me walk, | |
|  | He seemed to mutter words between his teeth. | 1330 |
|  | You'll pay for this! This hand's my guarantee.[26] | |
| Zeresh: | My friend, avenge yourself. Let the knave die. | |
|  | For him who sees you and won't humbly bow, | |
|  | Many horrible tortures ought to be prepared. | |
|  | For this fine Mordecai let a gallows be raised, | 1335 |
|  | Where in the sun his flesh can cook and dry out, | |
|  | Where the black blood seeps out for the curs to lick; | |
|  | Let no one dare to touch his hateful corpse | |
|  | To give it burial, and let the ravenous | |
|  | Hunger of cawing crows make it their meat; | 1340 |
|  | In short, let the bones, finally exposed, | |
|  | Be gnawed by foxes and devoured by wolves. | |
|  | Let the wooden gallows, fifty cubits high, | |
|  | Make it acknowledged by the crowds that gather | |
|  | How his vain pride, which of his life deprived him, | 1345 |
|  | Was raised no less high than his hanging body. | |
|  | Go to the king. Meanwhile, make preparation. | |
|  | You've nothing left to do but ask for it. | |
|  | He'll grant it to you; I firmly believe it. | |
| Haman: | I go. Let work begin with utmost speed. | 1350 |
|  | Before the sun goes to its watery bed, | |
|  | I'll make my knave a public spectacle. | |

(*Exeunt.*)

| | | |
|---|---|---|
| Chorus:[27] | "He's dead, poor fellow. It's too much presumption | |
|  | "To work against a prince by hook or crook. | |
|  | "In one of low degree nothing's less bearable | 1355 |
|  | "Than insolent pride; all laugh at him for that. | |
|  | "When one offends people who hold great power, | |
|  | "Disgrace is what may be received as payment. | |

(*Enter Ahasuerus.*)

Ahasuerus: "Grace, as they say, does not go without grace.
"It always turns its face toward its companion — 1360
"A sign that one should give and receive pleasures,
"And by this mutual action foster that desire.
"Each service rendered deserves recompense;
"And he who won't reward, thinking it would diminish
"His greatness, takes away from the well-wishers 1365
"The care that makes them more watchful for his welfare.
Since enjoyment of being alive is most
Precious, I wish to maintain all my days
The desire to keep near me, promote and honor
Those who've preserved me from so many snares. 1370
To whom then do I owe more than to this good
Mordecai, who with such care found out the treason
Of two accursed old men, two faithless eunuchs,
So that their cruel design against me failed?
At around midnight, since sweet slumber, whose 1375
Fluid makes human eyelids stick to eyes
And flows through hearts quite imperceptibly,
Didn't dull my senses with a gentle sprinkle,
By chance I start to read the chronicles
Where stories of my family are compiled. 1380
There, happening to find how this good old man
Had saved my life when it was in great danger
And that he failed to get a great reward,
I thought to myself: I must satisfy him,
Weighing his service by my lofty rank. 1385
"Each kindness bring at last sweet-smelling fruits;
"And if in early stages it brings none forth,
"It later will produce in more abundance.

(*Enter Haman.*)

But don't I see Haman? I want to award
By his advice a matchless honor to this Jew. 1390
Tell me, dear friend, what do we need to do
To honor someone more than normally?

Haman (*aside*): Some new and further triumph is prepared for
Me, and they want it to be of my choosing.[28]
(*aloud*) Your wisdom is so just and great, my prince, 1395

|             | That you should do no more but ask it of yourself;
For you distribute honor with proportion,
And not, like some men, solely by emotions.
However, since you ask what we need to do
To honor someone more than normally, | 1400 |
|             | May it please you clothe him in your robe of state,
Encircle his head with the royal crown,
And order further that he mount your horse;
Moreover, let the man you most esteem,
Walking alongside, use his hand to guide | 1405 |
|             | The fiery steed as it foams round the bit;
Let him go through the city in this fine attire,
And let a herald announce to city crowds:
See how this prince is honored by the king! | |
| Ahasuerus:  | Then do precisely that without delay | 1410 |
|             | To the old man Mordecai; in that way I
Am pleased clearly to show the love I bear him;
Let him drink in this honor; let his head be turned
By this choice glory. | |
| Haman:      | Well, it shall be done. | |

(*Exit King.*)

O rude command! What must I hope for, if                        1415
Against my plans, I must render an honor
Hardly fit for a king to my adversary?
Is that the gallows I was preparing for him?
Shall I go as herald, trumpeting the praise
Of him whom I just now viewed as a foreign slave?               1420
Of him whom I destined to die quite soon,
Since he at each meeting would not worship me?
O deceptive hope! Alas, I know too well
And to my cost the error that deceived my heart,
When I assured myself that the sought-for honor                 1425
Was offering itself; therefore, I tried
To make it excessive. But through you, false friend,
Alas, I contributed to my own shame!
"Mad is the man who trusts in a king's favor.
"One's greatest certainty is that he's faithless;               1430
"For he makes Fortune his confederate,
"And she'll set back the man who was advancing.

"May I descend from honor's summit freely,
"Rather than be hurled down to its abyss. (*Exit.*)

Chorus: "Fortune at court is similar to a wheel, 1435
"Whose highest point in one spin falls into the mud.
"He who's too puffed up with this worldly honor
"Will ultimately burst or be disgraced.

Chorus of Courtiers:[29]  Haman without doubt is beside himself.
See how he storms and seethes with rage, 1440
How his bile, swollen with black anger, tortures
Him, buffets him, hurls him continually,
How he fumes with passion, how his haughty head
Shakes his disordered locks, how he can't stand still.
His eye is flashing like a fiery omen 1445
Which once again clings to the firmament,
So as to threaten fields, cities and towns
With famine, pestilence and civil riots.
He can't contain his fury very long;
The storm might well reach even us. For what 1450
Can this innocent race have done, this good
And simple folk, timid and without malice,
Who, long held captive in this foreign clime,
Daily incur thousands of dangers here?
Indeed, they languish in a land so distant, 1455
They barely breathe amid so many sighs.
To please just Haman, with no cause or reason,
They want to exterminate this wretched house,
Or rather, this race with innumerable
Families dispersed throughout our major cities. 1460
"Thus are the lowliest injured by the great.
"To take away their means is not enough;
"But to put to death a whole people at once
"They deem a trifle; it's nothing to them;
"Though no one, even were he seated on the throne, 1465
"Could bring life back to just one of the slain.

(*Enter Messenger.*)

But don't I see someone running very swiftly?
Then let's walk up to him and learn why this
Haste. Stop, my friend, we wish to know what makes
You move so speedily upon your way. 1470

V.i.                  HAMAN

Messenger:[30]    I run toward Esther, our great princess, to
Tell her that Haman, followed by a crowd,
Is leading through the town with sovereign honor
Mordecai and guides his horse, holding the bridle.
They all, touched by humble respect, adore him;     1475
The royal robe and sceptre honor him;
A herald with loud voice proclaims before him:
Revere Mordecai, by order of the king of
Kings. Since you know all, I resume my voyage;
I have to bring this message to the queen.     1480

*(Exit.)*

Chorus:[31]    O change of fortune wholly unexpected!
The man who was despised is now seen honored;
The man who was adored is in turn despised!
"The grasp of fickle Fortune is unsteady;
"Her only constant is instability;     1485
"By her the man who seemed exalted is cast down,
"And he who was trampled in the mire is raised,
"When with a gentle shake she turns her wheel.
"Unhappy is he who relies on her
"Deceptive lures; she revels in our dangers!     1490

*(Enter Esther.)*

Esther:    At last then, flying above the clouds, my prayer
Has reached your ear, O King supreme. O you,
Who turn the hearts of rulers toward the goal
You wanted, whether men like it or not.
Then may thanks evermore be given to you;     1495
May your praise evermore be heard for this,
From eastern shore where the sun first lights its torch,
To the western sea where it's seen to go out.
You, having given impetus to this project,
Give me the courage to complete it well,     1500
So that this tyrant, this presumptuous man
Who steals your honor may have his degraded.
The king draws near; that puts my mind at ease.
I'll now prepare reproaches against Haman.

*(Enter Ahasuerus with Attendants.)*

Sole miracle of kings, both past and present,     1505

                I feel within my soul incredible
                Delight to have received by my good fortune
                The joy of being your moon, with you my sun.
                Great prince in whom my glory lies, oblige me
                By ordering Haman to come here at once.       1510
Ahasuerus:   Go fetch him then, since it pleases the queen.

                *(Exeunt Attendants.)*

                O sovereign lady of a sovereign king,
                O my sole love and my dearest desire,
                O my first pleasure and my final passion,
                You've so transported me by your extreme       1515
                Sweetness that now I'm yours more than I'm mine.
                Henceforth don't think that you can ask for something
                Which I would not be freely pleased to grant you.
                If we have but one heart, one soul in common,
                Let fortune also be common between us.       1520
Esther:      O great and worthy prince, to whom all mortals
                Deem themselves bound with lifelong duties, you
                Alone are my all, and I love my life
                Only to see my love followed by yours.
                Also, my glory lies in seeing myself       1525
                Serve to give pleasure to a king so great.
                May favoring Heaven be blessed always, for
                It caused my birth that I might see myself
                Nearly my master's mistress. From you both I get
                All kinds of gifts, without deserving them.       1530

                *(Enter Haman.)*

                But here's that Haman, that bloodthirsty tyrant
                Who, wishing to belie your normal gentleness
                And to abuse his authority by fraud,
                Against the rules of nations, against justice,
                Has vowed to wipe out all the Jews together—       1535
                No less than that, to sate his cruel rage;
                And thus involving in this common danger
                Your loyal Mordecai and your Esther, too.
                For this benevolent, obliging nation
                Gave to us both our name and origin.       1540
                But since he has brewed such a cruel plot
                Against you, against us, and your good subjects,

V.i. HAMAN 83

|              | May you be pleased to turn on his own head
|              | The harm he planned for us. Grant my request:
|              | May a whole guiltless people, in a foreign           1545
|              | Land, be by one man's death rescued from danger.
| Ahasuerus:   | You wretched slave, were you indeed so bold
|              | As to surprise me thus? Abuse my favor?
|              | Pursue and try to kill a queen, a people,
|              | Stating no reason, grievance, harm received?         1550
|              | You thus take pleasure in displeasing me?
|              | Go, ruffian, I sacrifice you to
|              | My harsh wrath, like a freed slave full of rashness,
|              | You who by false reports incensed me against Isaac.
|              | Remove him from my sight; cover his face.            1555
|              | Villain, this is your end; expect no pardon ever.
|              | I want to invent a new torture today
|              | Able to satisfy Esther my wife,
|              | The loyal Mordecai, his people and myself.
|              | To punish your sin it must be extreme.               1560

*(Exit Ahasuerus.)*[32]

| Haman:       | Treat me with mercy, formidable princess.
|              | I fall at your feet and implore you also:
|              | Look not on my fault, but on my repentance,
|              | And have my death sentence revoked. If you
|              | Make me so obligated to your greatness,              1565
|              | I'll be your very humble slave forever.
|              | "To pardon sinners who admit their errors,
|              | "Prostrate under the feet of lofty monarchs
|              | "And begging mercy with a stream of tears,
|              | "Is worthy of a woman and a queen.                   1570
|              | "The greatness of the sin recommends mercy.
|              | Madam, allow me to embrace your knees.

*(Reenter Ahasuerus with Mordecai.)*

| Ahasuerus:   | What, base, debauched man! To offend me's not enough;
|              | Before you die you want to force my wife!
|              | At once I'll take revenge so public that             1575
|              | After a thousand years it'll be remembered.
|              | Drag him away and hang him on the gallows
|              | That he'd reserved for my poor benefactor.[33]

*(Exeunt Attendants with Haman.)*

|            | And you, faithful old man, your race's glory, |      |
|            | Take up his honors and fill his position. | 1580 |
|            | As for you, my Esther, take possession of |      |
|            | His wealth, palace and slaves; I hold back nothing. |      |
|            | Let Haman's letters, skilfully contrived |      |
|            | To destroy the Jews, be speedily revoked.[34] |      |
|            | Let this people, more secure than ever, take | 1585 |
|            | Revenge on all its foes with impunity, |      |
|            | And, freed from crushing burdens of taxation,[35] |      |
|            | Breathe happily everywhere in this vast empire. |      |
| Mordecai:  | How well our kindly God had warned me that |      |
|            | His people one day would be rescued by you! | 1590 |
|            | Just when dawn scatters roses in the east |      |
|            | And doors are opened for the new sun to |      |
|            | Pursue its course through heaven's oblique expanse, |      |
|            | Two days ago a gentle sleep kept my eyes shut. |      |
|            | But lo! a horrid thunderstorm arises, | 1595 |
|            | The frightful noise of which makes the earth totter. |      |
|            | I see many whirlwinds spin above my head, |      |
|            | Many blazing lightning bolts pierce the dark sky, |      |
|            | And after them emerge from the clouds' belly |      |
|            | Numerous twinkling streaks of tiny sparks. | 1600 |
|            | Although my senses were gripped by great fear, |      |
|            | I saw, or so it seemed to me, two fierce dragons, |      |
|            | Their massive round forms crawling on the ground. |      |
|            | They raised their heads, to make war on each other, |      |
|            | Their eyes breathing with flame, their throats with wind. | 1605 |
|            | The trees around were shaking constantly, |      |
|            | And all the nearby area was shining |      |
|            | From the lustre that flashed from their slippery scales. |      |
|            | As loud a noise blared from their mighty voices |      |
|            | As tempests make when they uproot whole forests. | 1610 |
|            | At this noise I perceived everyone moving |      |
|            | Against the one race who rely on God. |      |
|            | The entire sky was covered with a sombre |      |
|            | Veil woven of black rain and shadowy mist. |      |
|            | Great streams of tears were flowing on the ground; | 1615 |
|            | The void was filling with sobs and alarms. |      |
|            | Then a weak people, harshly troubled, rendered |      |
|            | Dumbfounded by the violence of the torment, |      |

V.i. HAMAN 85

        Their crossed arms raised to heaven above their trembling
        Heads, waited for the horrid tempest's one blow.    1620
        But lo! as all their minds focused on God,
        A tiny spring of water started flowing,
        Which in an instant grows to such a river
        That its course waters all the countryside.
        The sun arises as its rays break through,    1625
        Dispersing all the mass of darkened mists.
        Then small men's humbleness is raised to heaven,
        And great men's arrogance is brought down to hell.
        At that point I awake and, recollecting
        The prophetic dream that wanders through my mind,    1630
        I probe at length for what God has determined;
        But I am baffled. Now that the outcome makes
        It clear, I fully recognize that what
        This vision showed me in masked form was no illusion.
        My mind grasps its entire intelligence,    1635
        Which I wish to present to you more clearly.
        The stream is Esther, and the sun's the king;
        The warring dragons are Haman against me;
        And the assembled crowds, stirred up to fight
        The friendless Jews, are the idolaters.    1640
        That the lowly are raised and the great brought low
        Is amply shown by my race and by Haman's.[36]
Esther:  O God, you never slumber for your people;
        You hold a vessel full of peerless favors,
        Another full of evils, which you pour upon us,    1645
        As we deserve your mercy or your anger.
        Grant that the holy race of saints may be
        Saved the same way in similar future dangers.

                (*Exeunt.*)

Chorus of the Faithful (adapted from Psalm 124):[37]
        Say, joyous Israel, had God not been for us,
        When numerous enemies afire with wrath    1650
        Were plotting all together to destroy us,
        We would have all been doomed; the abyss lay open,
        And its howling waves would have covered our heads
        To please a bloodthirsty tyrant's appetite.
        Just as a summer flood, swollen with streams,    1655

Carries off ripened wheat, bridges and shrubs,
Pushing its furious might in all directions,
The fury of many foreign peoples, joined
Confusedly, would thus have pillaged us,
And nothing would have stopped its hurtful rage.    1660
    But as this flood, so clamorous just now,
As it raced frantically across the earth,
Is so dried by the heat that not one wave
Remains, thus our foes, piled up on all sides,
Have been dispersed by one glance from the Lord,    1665
And not a single one of them appears now.
    Let's bless forever the eternal Lord
Who preserves his people with a father's care
And won't allow their race to fall a prey,
But on the contrary, makes their proud foes    1670
Subjected in disgrace to Israel's will;
All, wonder-struck by this, triumph in joy.
    Just as a bird, lured by the bird-catcher,
Escapes from the net spread for its destruction
And soars into the air, its flight unhindered,    1675
God has released us from the grasp that bound us.
Those who insulted us now wish us well;
Those who distressed us have consoled our hearts.
    May our aid always be from the God of Gods,
Who placed heaven's pavilion over the earth;    1680
We shall not lack hope or assurance, for
Although the whole world should take arms against us,
We have a shield that will fend off the blows,
A shield no human power can resist.

*END.*

## PERFIDY OF HAMAN, FAVORITE MINISTER OF KING AHASUERUS.

His conspiracy against the Jews, in which is seen realistically represented the wretched state of those who trust human greatness. The whole derived and extracted from the Old Testament Book of Esther.[38] With a pleasing and mirthful farce, taken from one of the gentlest wits of this age.

IN PARIS,

Printed by the Widow Ducarroy, rue des Carmes, at the sign of the Trinity.[39]

M. DC. XXII.

## Argument of the Tragedy.[40]

Fortune is so diversified in her effects that there is nothing settled or firm in the universe; everything that is under the sway and yoke of her laws is subject to changes, vicissitudes and inconstancy; nothing is found there except variety and mutability.

King Ahasuerus, the foremost monarch of the universe, had organized superb banquets in his city of Shushan to display his grandeur. There, while he was entertaining the company with his magnificence, Haman, his favorite, gave the command through the city that people bend the knee before him. Only Mordecai, uncle of Queen Esther, will not obey his commandment; Haman is informed of this and condemns all the Jews of the kingdom to death. Queen Esther, having learned of this through her uncle, was determined to save her people from this disaster; she comes to ask the King and his favorite to dine in her apartments, where after dinner she informs the King of the treason. The King, learning that the aforesaid Haman had had a gallows built to hang Mordecai (having two days previously had to bestow an honor upon the aforesaid Mordecai, for the conspiracy which he had formerly discovered), had the aforesaid Haman hanged on the very gallows which he had raised for Mordecai.

## The Names of the Characters.

KING AHASUERUS
QUEEN ESTHER
HAMAN           favorite
HARBONA
ZETHAR          princes
MORDECAI.
DURANDA       demon
SNATCH-SOUP
LICK-DISH
MARIOLE        executioner

# ACT I

(*Enter Ahasuerus, Zethar, Harbona.*)

Ahasuerus:  If ever the universe under the sway
          Of an earthly monarch trembled, if the sceptre
          Of kings preceding us ever had this power
          To break and tame the haughty arrogance
          Of earth and heaven, 'tis I who have the might    5
          To tame, break, overthrow, release and stop
          The force of mankind. Heaven, earth and sea
          Quake at my word. I need not go to war
          To impose my yoke; my voice makes each one tremble.
          I need but an instant to enforce my laws.    10
          The Scythians, Greeks, Moors, barbarians
          And those whom ocean separates from the mainland
          To me pay tribute; in short, everyone
          Whom the sun illumines with his fire-brand eye,
          Whether he leaves the sea to start his course    15
          Or turns his chariot and bridle back
          To end the day, no name is heard but that of
          Great Ahasuerus; his praise and renown
          From mouth to mouth and ear to ear do fly,
          Filling all mortal creatures with fresh wonder.    20
          Is there on earth a greater king than I?
          Who of the human race is not my subject?
          What living mortal does not fear my wrath?
          Who quakes not when I speak? I'm God on earth.
          Even the gods of heaven kneel to me,    25
          And if Jove ever angered me, I swear
          By Acheron, he'd feel my rage's force;[41]
          I'd swiftly make a slaughter of his gods.

|              | I don't much fear the thunderbolt he wields; |    |
|              | If he is armed with fire, my shield is bronze, | 30 |
|              | Which can withstand the assault of his cruel flame. |
|              | If his fist holds a lance, I've a new weapon |
|              | To raze or hack through anything. Lame Vulcan, |
|              | Dwelling in Hades, forged it with his hand. |
|              | In short, I fear not war, though Mars be for him. | 35 |
|              | If he is god above, I'm god on earth.[42] |
|              | All right, you, what report of my brave banquets? |
| Zethar:      | I swear, great King, that none has ever seen |
|              | Feasts of such splendor. |
| Harbona:     | 'Tis almost impossible |
|              | To do it justice. I think it exceeds | 40 |
|              | The powers of mortal man to tell its grandeur, |
|              | Whether for foods exquisite, fairest honors, |
|              | For fine provisions or for all the riches |
|              | Which dazzled the assembled Medes and Persians. |
| Zethar:      | Indeed, if I wished to recount the beauty | 45 |
|              | Of this rare banquet, I'd have sooner numbered |
|              | The sands that pile up on the sandy shores |
|              | When Neptune makes the mutinous waves to swell. |
| Harbona:     | Indeed, I'd sooner have counted the bright torches |
|              | That light the heavens when the steeds divine | 50 |
|              | Of Phoebus, panting from his fiery heat, |
|              | Drown daylight calm beneath the sparkling sea. |
| Ahasuerus:   | The plan for this proud banquet I conceived |
|              | Some time ago; my heart spurred on with hopes |
|              | To make my fame resound, always desired | 55 |
|              | To stage this feast at some point in my life.[43] |
| Zethar:      | I promise, Sire, that centuries to come |
|              | Will sing your praises; the remembrance of |
|              | This gallant feast and of your bounteous glory |
|              | Shall ever be inscribed in Memory's temple. | 60 |
| Harbona:     | How beautiful it was! On one side were |
|              | The lords and princes glittering and bright |
|              | Like fairest suns, and their embroidered robes |
|              | Were woven from beneath with precious stones. |
|              | All was perfumed with the divinest scents; | 65 |
|              | The tapestries enriched with heavenly colors, |
|              | Forming pavilions, surrounded all the guests. |

|            | These marvels filled the courtiers all with wonder. |     |
|            | Elsewhere the silver and the golden plates |     |
|            | Shone from all sides. This vast, rich treasure | 70 |
|            | From cities of the realm gathered in one place |     |
|            | Would often dazzle the beholders' eyes. |     |
|            | In another corner lutes, cornets and oboes, |     |
|            | With fifes and drums and wondrous vocalists,[44] |     |
|            | Joining together in their diverse songs | 75 |
|            | Swept all the Medes and Persians off their feet. |     |
| Zethar: | But you say nothing of the haute cuisine |     |
|            | Served there; indeed, I guarantee that never |     |
|            | Have such delicacies of meat been seen, |     |
|            | So succulent, so tender, so enticing. | 80 |
|            | One saw there a parade of partridges, |     |
|            | Capons, hares, rabbits for dainty gourmets. |     |
|            | The next course, venison, was standing guard, |     |
|            | The does and deer, sliced up in a round pie, |     |
|            | Made the rounds all over, while the drinking goblets, | 85 |
|            | Ingeniously engraved with artful skill |     |
|            | By the forger god, made in the shape of vases, |     |
|            | Filled with fine wine were passed to all and sundry. |     |
|            | In short, 'twas all so fair that in trying to tell |     |
|            | The slightest part of the feast I'm at a loss, | 90 |
|            | My mind keeps straying, and when I compare |     |
|            | My recollections with my words, I see |     |
|            | I rather have diminished than extolled |     |
|            | This banquet rich here in this royal park. |     |
| Ahasuerus: | All would have gone well had my proud wife shown | 95 |
|            | Obedience, thus averting the rebuke |     |
|            | She merited. How strange a case it is |     |
|            | That a wife will not obey the King, her husband. |     |
|            | I'd summoned her so that all present might |     |
|            | In deep humility adore her beauty, | 100 |
|            | So that she'd come display her costly garments, |     |
|            | Her robe, her jewels and her fair ornaments. |     |
|            | And yet the impudent creature had no shame, |     |
|            | She showed contempt for me, defied my order. |     |
|            | Ler her no more be mentioned, I never want | 105 |
|            | To see her more; she has failed her duty too much. |     |
|            | Besides, thank god, I have another mistress |     |

|   |   |   |
|---|---|---|
| | Who in riches and praise surpasses Vashti. | |
| | I wish to make her Queen; let first of all | |
| | My Princes on their knees before her fall.[45] | 110 |
| Harbona: | Sire, I affirm to you that she's a goddess | |
| | In beauty excelling, for, to start, her tresses | |
| | Which rustle in the gentle, wafting breezes | |
| | Are at their peak adorned with richest diamonds | |
| | That Ganges ever bore; her lustrous face, | 115 |
| | Perfumed with lilies and with fragrant roses, | |
| | Attracts all mortals with its glow divine; | |
| | Her mouth is coral, and the fair vermilion | |
| | Of her red lips is sprinkled with fresh roses | |
| | Ever in full bloom, with no fear of winter, | 120 |
| | Her manner stern yet sweet, her speech divine. | |
| | Her hair is light brown, pale red her complexion; | |
| | Her two eyes flashing with a mighty light | |
| | Surpass by far the rays of early dawn. | |
| | To sum up, I believe she is some Venus | 125 |
| | Who with her radiance captivates your heart.[46] | |
| Ahasuerus: | I wish henceforth that she be crowned with state | |
| | Queen of the Orient, since her destiny | |
| | Has led her hither. This is my desire, | |
| | My full intent; such is our royal pleasure. | 130 |

*(Enter Esther.)*

|   |   |   |
|---|---|---|
| Zethar: | O Sire, behold the Queen, she brings some news. | |
| Ahasuerus: | Come in, Madam, come in, come in, young damsel. | |
| | Banish all fear. | |
| Esther: | Forgive me, Sire, for daring | |
| | To show myself before so great a King. | |
| Ahasuerus: | Now really, do you think a murderous tigress | 135 |
| | Suckled and raised me, or that I'm so dreadful | |
| | From deeds of war that no one dares approach me? | |
| | No, no, I'm not a hard, unyielding rock. | |
| | "A King should be sweet and benign by nature. | |
| | "These virtues are the ornament rich and fair | 140 |
| | He should be clothed in; ask with confidence | |
| | Whatever you desire, and tell me plainly | |
| | What makes your heart sad; I swear, Prince's honor, | |
| | That even if you sought the finest province | |

|  |  |  |
|---|---|---|
|  | In all my empire, you at once would have it, | 145 |
|  | For you have always pleased me most of all. |  |
| Esther: | O Sire, great Emperor, who halts the winds, |  |
|  | Even the fierce north winds with but one word, |  |
|  | I have one matter to request and tell you; |  |
|  | I beg today that you grant my petition; | 150 |
|  | If I have any strength and have found favor |  |
|  | In the sweet sight of your most august face, |  |
|  | Do me this honor, you and your favorite, |  |
|  | To come today for supper to my table |  |
|  | In my pavilion, where your humble servant | 155 |
|  | Prepares for you a feast with cheer and mirth. |  |
| Ahasuerus: | Yes, darling, we'll attend; farewell, be at rest. |  |
|  | I swear, King's honor, that I never saw |  |
|  | A woman who pleased me half as much as you. |  |
|  | We'll come; farewell then. Order all things well. | 160 |

(*Exeunt all but Esther.*)

| | | |
|---|---|---|
| Esther: | O mighty God, ruler of heaven and earth, |  |
|  | You who set bounds to the paths of shining stars, |  |
|  | Who cause the sea to swell, whose power can crush |  |
|  | Man's arrogance in the twinkling of an eye, |  |
|  | 'Tis this day I have set aside, great God, | 165 |
|  | To give you thanks for having raised me up |  |
|  | To this high, honored rank—me, a poor girl |  |
|  | From a foreign country and a foreign city, |  |
|  | Of Hebrew ancestry, who for one year |  |
|  | Have dwelt with my captive race in Shushan here. | 170 |
|  | Our hope, great Monarch, and all our confidence |  |
|  | We always, sensibly, have placed in you. |  |
|  | 'Tis you who, from of old, cherish the Hebrews; |  |
|  | 'Tis you who make them blessed above all peoples. |  |
|  | You saved them long ago from extermination | 175 |
|  | By drowning Pharaoh, all his host and chariots; |  |
|  | You fed them in the wilderness with manna |  |
|  | From heaven for the space of forty years. |  |
|  | Therefore, O great Prime Mover, I now implore |  |
|  | Your aid divine, on this day I adore | 180 |
|  | Your majesty and your omnipotence. |  |
|  | I appeal, O Lord, to your benevolence. |  |

May it please you to grant me my petition.
Avert, great God, the dire catastrophe
That looms over the Jews. 'Tis cruel Haman, 185
Filled with ambition; he's the odious tyrant
Who has destined us for slaughter, sack and pillage.
Avert then, O my God, this dreadful carnage;
Restore the people to full liberty,
So that, in time to come, by your decree 190
They'll praise your name and gracious power with song
For humbling the fierce arrogance of the strong.

*(Exit.)*

# ACT II

*(Enter Duranda.)*

Duranda: In Hades have I stayed far, far too long.[47]
Too long I've languished, too long irons borne.
Henceforth I must all over freely roam.  195
Too hard I've worked; I need to catch my breath.
I'm a poor devil, and they ought to whip me.
I waste my time rubbing an ass's head,
Rogue that I am, with boiling laundry lye.[48]
But meantime I've forgot Pluto's express  200
Missive I'm to dispatch, fooling around
With a poor sheep's skin, while the hungry flock
Is fleeing far from us.[49] Alas, poor wretch,
I ought to hide my face, I'm no good devil.
Why work for Hades, just to die from hunger?  205
No drinking there, no eating, meatless, breadless–
A great place, really: everything in chaos.
At times not even a single bone to gnaw.
I sometimes was constrained to dine on snakes,
In lieu of decent food. Do I regret that!  210
At times I had to drink wind on a rock.
Then down I'd have to go to turn the spit
Of all-devouring Pluto. But the worst of it
Was: never dared I taste these salmagundies.
Pluto eats all alone; when he's at table,  215
You'd swear it was a pig inside a stable:
He wallows, stuffs himself and whets his teeth.
At last he even forbids his staff to enter.
If any scales remain, his mouth he widens;
His two hands shove from the ladle into his "oven."  220

No KP needed there; his platters always
Are clean. No spheres in space, but clearest plates.[50]
But that's not all; what really makes me mad
Is: never did they give me one hour's rest,
For when one chore was done, without a pause     225
Another labor came to take its place.
At times old Cerberus, three-headed hound,
And keeper of the gate, would order me
To take its place, so that meanwhile this dog
Could gobble Stygian Pluto's banquet trays.      230
At times I was compelled to carry a stone
From vale to mountain top, then it would fall
And my painful labor started once again.[51]
Now cast into a fire, now plunged in streams,
Always at work, now poking up the flames         235
Of boiling cauldrons, full of men and women.
At last, when I saw so many new arrivals
In death's dark realm, and sure my non-stop life
Was not the best kind, I employed deceit.
One day as Pluto, throbbing in his glee,         240
Was dining in his palace, I went straight
To Charon's boat, where he sat, oar in hand.
I ordered him to ferry me across,
For Hades' lord had sent me with a message.
Immediately he asked me for a passport;          245
Sans passport I would not get to the shore.
Said he: "I make no inquiry of your voyage.
Give me a passport, I'll take you across.
But you're the master liar, too well we know you.
Your knaveries could make me rue the day."       250
Was I amazed! For Orcus' river broad[52]
Prevented me from turning back. At last,
Remembering that I possessed the seal
Of Pluto, locked up in my little parcel,
I hand it over, cross the Styx and journey on,   255
Arriving in this land with joy and gladness.
You may be sure I'll never again set foot there.
I much prefer to dwell in joy right here.
Wouldn't I be stupid to go back to torment
Since now I have the means to live in comfort?   260

Already I've a house and sure position:
I'll stay with Haman; he shall be my master,
For he loves honors, and his soul's inflated
With pride and arrogance — that's my guarantee,
Just what I need. The King has made him great      265
In praise and honors, his the highest rank
Among the lords. He's now within my reach;
I have to catch him, so his soul entrapped
In my deceiving nets may pay me tribute.
When I have served him here (this is my goal),      270
How sweet 'twill be to see him in my cauldron,
Where front and back I'll turn him on a spit.
A gallows has he made, but I'm afraid
He'll be the first to test the gallows' height.
He thinks he's towering, but perhaps the noose      275
Will soon increase the tallness of his frame.
But not a word more, silence, here comes Haman.
I ask you, is he not a gallant courtier?[53]

*(Exit Duranda; enter Haman.)*

Haman:  Peer to the King I walk, and the bright sun[54]
Proclaims my glory from the Orient      280
Unto the Ocean; Ganges' shores obey me;
The Tagus fears my law; the sound of my
Proud voice sets Pactolus' gold head atremble,
To plunge again at once beneath the waves.
The peoples of the East, the Moors, the Greeks,      285
The Persians are compelled to heed my voice.
Great general am I amidst the armies;
Of naught but my great name and fame men speak.
The princes, nobles, grandees of the court
Kneel down before me, each of them in turn.      290
I am the favorite of great Ahasuerus.
All people fear my word, all men revere me.
My name is everywhere, all sing my praises.
Yet with all this I do not feel at ease.
A certain Mordecai above all ires me,      295
Makes fun of me and pushes me aside,
Treats me like scum. But in the next few days[55]
I'll make him feel the pangs of sad remorse.

The gallows is all ready, he must dwell there.
Let him be hanged thereon within this hour! 300
Great Ahasuerus expressly has commanded
That I be adored like him. This man alone
Despises his decree. 'Tis time to punish
This Jew's fell crime. I mean to have him hanged.

*(Enter Mordecai.)*

Ah, scoundrel, there you are! What made you dare 305
To set foot here? Are you not faint with fear?

Mordecai: What means this terrifying man today
Who thinks to scare me with his fearsome voice?
Have you had one drink too many? You're insane.
Does no man dare present himself before you? 310

Haman: Quite so, but don't you know the King's command
That subjects must adore me or be hanged?
Yet you still dare appear erect before me!
I'll teach you to despise the King, and soon.

Mordecai: O what a prince! Adore a man like you? 315
I'd rather worship a mere apple stalk.
Is it not splendid that a mere carpenter,
That a plebeian should receive such honor?
You ought to hide your face.

Haman: By the King I swear
That you shall shortly see my direst vengeance. 320
I leave at once. Your gallows is all ready.
Today I must accomplish what I wish for.

*(Exit Haman.)*

Mordecai: Beware yourself that, having made the scaffold,
Yourself today will be impaled upon it.
How strange it is that a miniscule ant 325
Should build himself this day a royal pavilion—
A little servant acting like the master
And showing off in front of all the nobles!
He makes men honor him, takes a royal title.
On seeing him you'd say: a worthy lord. 330
Now if he really were of noble race,
I'd say: with cause is he puffed up with pride.
But this is a mere commoner, a knave.
Was not his father an impoverished tailor?[56]

He says he has a gallows built to hang me.  335
But I'm not very scared; he can't surprise me.
The Queen's my cousin; she can turn aside
This danger and make it redound on him.
Then let's go boldly: should the King seize me,
The Queen will help me, pleading tenderly.[57]  340

*(Exit.)*

# Interlude[58]

(*Enter Snatch-Soup.*)

Snatch-Soup: Aha, here's just the thing, this will be dinner.
    Good Sirs, don't breathe a word. This is for breakfast.
    I must hide it well; by chance if someone found it,
    I'd have to look for fodder somewhere else.

(*Enter Lick-Dish.*)

Lick-Dish: Snatch-Soup, come here. Where did you put the platter
    That you had in your hands? The King was looking.   346
    No lying now. If it's here in the larder,
    Be sure it will soon see a royal supper.[59]
    I know you've always been a clever rogue.
    The other day I saw you pinch a plump   350
    Capon from the feast.

Snatch-Soup:               By Hades' mouth I swear
    I have no platter. Rather may the cavern
    Of Pluto swallow me, and my poor self
    Henceforth reside in the kingdom of the dead.

Lick-Dish: All right, but that's not all. Is your soup made?   355
    We still must dine, for otherwise our strength
    Would fail us on the way.

Snatch-Soup:              All is prepared.
    But tell me, please, have you put nothing by?

Lick-Dish: I've set aside nothing but three full bottles
    Of excellent white wine, the very best.   360

Snatch-Soup: That's really great. We must get out of here
    And with a capon quickly drink it down.

Lick-Dish: Not so fast. Always arid is your throat.
    Don't hurry so much, you are far too greedy.
    You love white wine.

Snatch-Soup:             And claret just as much.   365

Lick-Dish: Always gorging yourself, but never a care
    For your poor starving children and your wife

|                | Who wastes away. You treat her shamelessly. |
|---|---|
| Snatch-Soup: | O worthy personage! One would say on seeing him: |
| | Here is a doctor filled with erudition! 370 |
| Lick-Dish: | Am I, like you, constantly seen in taverns? |
| | Have I been carried home from there with lanterns, |
| | Staggering through the streets? Where were you last night, |
| | When you were short of cash to pay the barman? |
| Snatch-Soup: | Poor Lick-Dish, you are not, alas, a drinker. 375 |
| | It grieves me so! But where's your memory? |
| | You'd dare not dip your fingers in it, say you? |
| | It's you who call me with you when you drink! |
| | But come here please, since I must tell you all. |
| | To hear you talk, you hardly dare to laugh. 380 |
| | Where were you the other day when, oh so jolly, |
| | You'd spent the final farthing that you owned? |
| | Your gait was tottering, and you did capers. |
| | Your wanton stares showed people, at a distance, |
| | How loose your noggin rested on your shoulder. 385 |
| | All you yourself do is drink night and day. |
| Lick-Dish: | All right, but when I drink, do you pay for me? |
| | I think, when I see you, good, worthy fellow, |
| | That though you'd five or six gold bars for payment, |
| | That wouldn't square your debt; you'd still owe more. 390 |
| | Therefore, you're always joyless and in torment, |
| | With never a penny to your name. For me, |
| | When you see me go to the cabarets, |
| | They never confiscate my coat as forfeit. |
| | I always come out quits by paying the hostess, 395 |
| | But *you* pay always with cold promises. |
| | Beware of officers! All right, drop the subject. |
| Snatch-Soup: | Let's speak of food; we've put it off too long. |
| | You say you've stashed away three or four bottles. |
| | Come, I'll show you a dish that's fit for kings. 400 |
| Lick-Dish: | I knew it. You've been stealing from the feast. |
| | Watch out or you'll end up by being caught. |
| Snatch-Soup: | Let's hurry off. I heard someone on the stairs. |
| Lick-Dish: | Let's go. Make sure they don't catch us unawares. |

(*Exeunt.*)

# ACT III

*(Enter Ahasuerus, Harbona, Zethar.)*

Ahasuerus: We've banqueted too long. 'Tis time to think 405
About affairs of state, for if some danger
Chanced to surround us during this assembly,
Our city would be shortly plunged in turmoil.
Harbona, tell me, have the people grumbled?
Have you seen anyone who has been angered 410
By my fine banquets?
Harbona: Sire, all of your empire
For eight days now has seen continuous joy.
At court the princes have abstained from quarrels.
Indeed, who could wish to overthrow your reign?
Zethar: However, yesterday I received word 415
Of rioting throughout the town of Turd.
But, as I have heard since, your governor
Has quelled the fighting. At his voice the people
Became more docile.
Ahasuerus: Truly I'm delighted
That he could calm that cruel public disturbance. 420
You always find someone lurking in ambush.
I was quite sure my banquets would not finish
Without some fighting, and the rabble's heart
Would be puffed up with boldness and contention.
But since my kingdom is at peace now, I 425
Inquire no more. I swear and promise you
That so long as the Fates spin out my life
And savage destiny has not snatched it away,
Peace is assured, and the fair golden age
Shall be reborn herein with all its splendor. 430

## III. PERFIDY OF HAMAN

|  |  |  |
|---|---|---|
|  | Henceforth, I trust, we shall learn how to live. |  |
|  | Enough talk, though. Fetch me the chronicles, |  |
|  | The record of my predecessors' deeds, |  |
|  | This book which can enlighten our successors. |  |
| Harbona: | Sire, here's the book. |  |
| Ahasuerus: | Come closer. Someone read it. | 435 |
|  | Let's see if it contains some glorious action. |  |
|  | Open at random, read the text aloud. |  |
| Harbona: | 'Tis done, Sire, now I'll read at your command. |  |
|  | "Chapter where Mordecai averts the treason |  |
|  | Of Teresh and Bigthan,[60] discovering | 440 |
|  | Their vicious plot to slay the Emperor |  |
|  | And seize from him his goods, his life and honor." |  |
| Ahasuerus: | I like this chapter very much, read on. |  |
|  | This happened, I recall, in my ornate room. |  |
| Harbona: | "Bigthan and Teresh, seeing that Ahasuerus | 445 |
|  | The King was all alone in his glorious house, |  |
|  | Conspired to kill him, but good Mordecai |  |
|  | Found out the plot, and filled with indignation |  |
|  | That these two subjects, whom our great King never |  |
|  | Would have suspected, without fear or scruple | 450 |
|  | Had sworn between them to destroy and slay |  |
|  | The King and other lords of this proud empire —[61] |  |
|  | When Mordecai had seen how great a crime |  |
|  | They planned, in league against his Majesty, |  |
|  | He warned the Queen, and she immediately, | 455 |
|  | Entering the room wherein the King was walking, |  |
|  | Warned the Emperor, and thus the criminals |  |
|  | Were sent before their time to Hades' shores." |  |
| Ahasuerus: | Stop, don't go on. What was the recompense |  |
|  | Bestowed on him who gave me timely warning? | 460 |
| Harbona: | He never, Sire, received any reward. |  |
|  | Remaining in your court, he seems abandoned |  |
|  | By gods and men. |  |
| Ahasuerus:[62] | I tell you and I swear it |  |
|  | That I shall honor him within this hour. |  |
|  | Go see without, and bring inside to me | 465 |
|  | One of my nobles. I wish to remember |  |
|  | This good Mordecai. |  |
| Zethar: | Indeed, Sire, he deserved |  |

To gain an honor worthy of his merits.

*(Enter Haman.)*

Haman: Sire, I have come; you had me summoned here.
 I would not have wished longer to delay. 470
Ahasuerus: Haman, approach, tell me, what must I do
 To one I like and who aims to delight me?
 Tell me what honors ought to be bestowed,
 Tell how he might above all be revered.
Haman: The man, Sire, who has found some favor in 475
 The sweet aspect of your most august face
 Should be adorned with glory and the royal mantle,
 Your sceptre in his hand, and your own horse
 Should be his mount, so that he may be known
 As greatest lord of all the nobility. 480
 Further, some prince or other noble lord
 Must serve him as herald to proclaim his honor,
 And thus covered with glory, amidst the city
 He'll make his subtle power felt everywhere.[63]
Ahasuerus: Go then, make haste and do as you have said, 485
 My royal mantle and my richest garment take
 And honor Mordecai, so that the youth
 Living in Shushan may admire his valor.
Haman: O wretched me, have I so loyal been
 To be surmounted by a mortal foe? 490

*(Exit Haman; enter Esther.)*[64]

Esther: Great Emperor, who with your might surmount
 The lofty arrogance of wicked men,
 Forgive me, Sire, if I dare enter here;
 My heart and mind are paralyzed with fear.
Ahasuerus: Arise, my goddess and my spouse divine, 495
 What news have you to tell? Is something wrong?
 What brings you here? I pledge my kingly word,
 I love your name more dearly than my own.
 Ask me, I'll grant it. Tell me why such sorrow
 Now fills your heart with bitterness and distress. 500
 I'll set it all to rights; do you not know
 That I am yours until death do us part,
 And that sooner will the sun desert his path
 Than I will change my prime affection for you?

## III. PERFIDY OF HAMAN

|  | Speak then, I pray you, whence comes this affliction, | 505 |
|---|---|---|
|  | These sighs and moans that torture your sad heart? |  |
| Esther: | Sire, 'tis today that one of your grandees |  |
|  | With haughty envy shall destroy our lives. |  |
|  | I and my people have been marked for slaughter, |  |
|  | For sack and pillage, and the day appointed | 510 |
|  | To perform this massacre will soon arrive,[65] |  |
|  | In which you'll see, ere long, a dreadful plot. |  |
|  | Alas, great Emperor, will you have the heart |  |
|  | To view this tempest and this cruel carnage? |  |
|  | Would your heart be calm as you see me expire | 515 |
|  | By tyrants' hands, and raise no opposition? |  |
|  | I beg you, then, great King, if holy affection |  |
|  | Is still engraved within your gracious breast, |  |
|  | If my love moves you and the sacred respect |  |
|  | I bear you still has any small effect, | 520 |
|  | I beg today that you drive back the storm |  |
|  | That threatens to engulf me and my people. |  |
| Ahasuerus: | And who would make so bold to threaten you? |  |
|  | Who among humans dares so far transgress |  |
|  | My edict? I cannot believe my kingdom | 525 |
|  | Shall ever endure a man so impudent. |  |
| Esther: | Alas, Sire, yet it's one of your grandees |  |
|  | Who has consigned us all to myriad torments. |  |
| Ahasuerus: | One of my nobles, say you! Which one is he? |  |
| Esther: | 'Tis cruel Haman before whom all men bow. | 530 |
| Ahasuerus: | Haman? I don't believe it. |  |
| Esther: | Sire, he has sent |  |
|  | To all your provinces word to join forces |  |
|  | Against me and my people, authorized |  |
|  | By your official seal as firm assurance |  |
|  | To slay us all.[66] |  |
| Ahasuerus: | By Acheron I swear | 535 |
|  | That he'll receive, ere long, his just reward. |  |
| Esther: | Sire, here he comes. |  |

*(Enter Haman.)*

| Ahasuerus: | Approach, you reckless man. |
|---|---|
|  | Whence comes your boldness? Are you so audacious |
|  | To plot against my state and undertake |

|  |  |  |
|---|---|---|
|  | To betray my wife and take me by surprise? | 540 |
|  | Your crime is flagrant; I shall have your head. |  |
|  | Aha! is't thus he treats me like his toy? |  |
| Zethar: | Sire, that's not all. He has built a strappado |  |
|  | To trap Mordecai during his walk and hang him. |  |
| Ahasuerus:[66] | Can this be true? Ah! wretched, wicked man, | 545 |
|  | You forgot yourself too far, you rose too high. |  |
|  | Hang him at once; let this be his reward, |  |
|  | For building his own gibbet in his lifetime. |  |
| Haman: | Ah, Madam, plead, implore him for my life! |  |
|  | Must I then end my days so miserably? | 550 |
| Ahasuerus: | Indeed! You make so bold to address my wife? |  |
|  | Let's go, my sweet, and leave this infamous man. |  |

(*Exeunt all but Haman.*)

| | | |
|---|---|---|
| Haman:[66] | Oh Sire, oh Sire! Alas, what, must I die? |  |
|  | Forgive, I beg you. What, must I expire |  |
|  | Upon a gallows? Gods, what a reward | 555 |
|  | For having served the King, helped to defend |  |
|  | Kingdom and state. Oh gods, how rigorous, |  |
|  | What cruelty stern, what frightful horror is this! |  |
|  | Then I must die. |  |

(*Enter Executioner; gallows is revealed.*)

| | | |
|---|---|---|
| Executioner (*holding out the noose*): | The matter is resolved. |  |
|  | Yes, you must die. Hey, look, the King sends greetings. | 560 |
|  | It's your last collar. Move, it's getting late. |  |
| Haman: | I beg you, hangman, have more consideration |  |
|  | For me than other men. Alas, how bitter! |  |
|  | At least, since I must die, had I a pen,[67] |  |
|  | I would write my wife. Alas, so high I soared | 565 |
|  | Above all men! Now wretched fate assaults me. |  |
| Executioner: | Come, come, don't be afraid, take heart a bit. |  |
|  | I'll make you taller; it's to your advantage. |  |
|  | You'll be raised fifteen feet above the ground, |  |
|  | Whereas you used to be but five feet high.[68] | 570 |
|  | Is it not logical that he who orders built |  |
|  | Some noble lodging, and wishes to enjoy it, |  |
|  | Should mount from floor to floor and gaze at leisure |  |
|  | On all features that suit him, give him pleasure? |  |
|  | 'Tis you who had this gallows fair erected. | 575 |

|            | Come on, start walking. 'Tis time you reflected: |     |
|            | Is't big enough? We'll try it out on you, |     |
|            | And in this place you'll stay the winter through. |     |
| Haman:     | O woe is me, how miserable am I! |     |
|            | Today I must become a laughingstock, | 580 |
|            | Exposed, alas, to all, in this fine array. |     |
|            | Would that my soul didn't feel such bitter struggling! |     |
|            | If the King had me beheaded, like a noble, |     |
|            | I would not dread so much the storm and fury |     |
|            | That shortly must pour down upon my head. | 585 |
|            | But what fills me with pain, dismay and dread |     |
|            | Is that I'm forced to use the very gallows |     |
|            | That I myself had raised at my expense. |     |
|            | Alas, my poor wife and my ten poor sons, |     |
|            | What will you say to see my limbs decaying, | 590 |
|            | From a gibbet dangling? O thou strumpet Fortune, |     |
|            | Thou'rt like the waves of Neptune's raging sea, |     |
|            | Which one moment toss the ship up toward the skies, |     |
|            | And hurtle it the next toward Hades' lair. |     |
|            | I once found favor in the eyes of the King; | 595 |
|            | Today, alas, I have lost everything. |     |
|            | Oh gods, what torments! |     |
| Executioner: | Babbling, time you waste.[69] |     |
|            | Away, enough of talk. *I* must make haste. |     |
| Haman:     | Farewell heaven and earth, farewell poor wife, |     |
|            | Farewell small children; lead a blameless life. | 600 |

*(Exeunt.)*

THE END

## NOTES TO THE TEXT

1. Atlas, who joined the revolt of the giants against the gods, was condemned to bear the weight of the heavens on his shoulders. Haman enjoys thinking of himself as mightier than the Titans (cf. vv. 382–84).
2. The terms "relent" and "puant" (both translated as "stinking"), which would be rejected as undignified by later generations of French poets, were still deemed acceptable for the lofty style of tragedy and epic in Montchrestien's day.
3. This is the first of many examples of the extended simile, in which a human action is compared to something in the world of nature, with the image often developed at length. The technique, more suited to epic, had been used by Seneca and was widely imitated in the works of Renaissance playwrights.
4. The unusual metaphor, while not directly derived from the Bible, may have been inspired by passages such as this: "transgressors have reached their full measure" (Daniel 8.23).
5. Seiver notes the similarity between the ideas expressed in vv. 320–22 and Psalm 72.
6. Vv. 417–60 provide a good example of the rhetorical technique of amplificatio: Montchrestien constructs a long speech by elaborating on the ideas found in the brief corresponding speech in the Bible (Esther 3.8–9).
7. Haman is surprisingly well informed about Jewish history in the period of Moses and Joshua.
8. The idea that the gods were invented by human rulers in order to force their subjects into obedience to the laws has a very long history. Sextus Empiricus quotes a passage from an early Greek poet named Critias which makes a similar argument (*Adversus Mathematicos* 9.54).
9. Seiver notes a parallel with Lamentations 3.45.
10. The sense of the expression *dépêcher le paquet à mon homme* is not fully clear. I think that "my man" refers to Mordecai. The verb *dépêcher* in that period had among its meanings "to get rid of, to send to execution." The word *paquet* could mean "attack," as in the expressions "dresser un paquet" and "adresser un paquet" noted in Huguet's dictionary.
11. The allusion to Matthew 7.3 is one of the rare uses of New Testament imagery in the play.
12. Seiver notes the parallel with Job 3.11.
13. Vv. 679–740 are an amplification of Mordecai's prayer in the apocryphal portion of the Book of Esther (13.9–17).
14. Vv. 733–36 were possibly inspired by Psalm 115.17–18.
15. Sarah and Rachel, the queen's two attendants, are apparently Jewish and know of their mistress's relationship to Mordecai. According to ancient Jewish legend, Esther surrounded herself with Jewish maidens (as will be the case in Racine's *Esther*).

16 Vv. 803–32 are based on the queen's prayer in the apocryphal portion of Esther (14.15–18).
17 This reaction of the Jews of Shushan is also mentioned in the Apocrypha (13.18).
18 This hymn (vv. 879–934) is a close adaptation of Psalm 79, with one stanza per Biblical verse. The reference to Haman replaces a more general reference to "neighbors," and vv. 919–22 are an interpolation.
19 Montchrestien is taking some liberties with Biblical history, according to which the Temple was destroyed by the Babylonian army under Nebuchadnezzar.
20 The shepherd boy is, of course, David.
21 Based on Exodus Chapter 3.
22 Vv. 1068–84 are an expansion of Mordecai's speech in Esther 4.13–14. There is no mention of the three days of fasting and prayer that preceded the queen's mission to her husband. If, as Seiver thought, Montchrestien was consciously trying to observe the unity of time, the omission is deliberate.
23 This eloquent passage is one of the play's few explicit references to Christianity.
24 The majority of this scene (Esther's entry supported by two maids, her fainting, the king's comforting words, and her comparing him to an angel) is derived from the apocryphal portion of Esther, Chapter 15.
25 While the names of all the confidants in the play were supplied by Montchrestien, Arphaxat is a rather surprising choice. Arphaxad (to use the Vulgate's spelling) was the son of Shem and grandson of Noah (Genesis 11.10).
26 Vv. 1293–1331 are an amplification of Esther 5.11,13.
27 If Griffiths is correct, then this is the commentator chorus speaking, in which case "poor fellow" refers to Haman and the "prince" is Ahasuerus. But if this is a group of Haman's friends, then "poor fellow" refers to Mordecai and "prince" to Haman.
28 This aside is based on Esther 6.6.
29 Montchrestien does not specify the identity of this chorus, which must be distinct from the commentator chorus that speaks at v. 1435, but it is clearly a character chorus, since it will converse with a solo character. That this is not a chorus of Jews is evident from vv. 1451–56.
30 A messenger who, like this one, brings good tidings rather than bad, is a rarity in tragedy.
31 If Griffiths is correct, this speech belongs to the commentator chorus, but it could just as logically be spoken by the chorus of courtiers.
32 Montchrestien does not indicate, as does the Bible (Esther 7.7), that the king goes out into the garden at this point. But if the king remains on stage during Haman's plea for mercy, there is no logical explanation for

his mistaken assumption that Haman is trying to force the queen.

33  Since Montchrestien has eliminated the intervention of the chamberlain Harbona who informs the king about the gallows which Haman prepared for Mordecai (Esther 7.9), it is not clear how the king could have learned about it.

34  In the Bible this is not possible, since the Persian legal system made all royal decrees irrevocable. The best Ahasuerus can do is to issue a second decree ordering the Jews to fight back on the day designated for their extermination.

35  The Bible notes that Ahasuerus imposed a tribute upon the land (10.1). Seiver suggests that Montchrestien may have known the Targum, which specifies that the Jews were exempted from that tax.

36  The dream and its interpretation are taken from the Apocrypha (11.5–11 and 10.4–9). However, Mordecai had that dream long before the events of the play, during the second year of the king's reign (11.2). Perhaps the change is due to Montchrestien's desire to observe the unity of time.

37  Montchrestien himself specifies the source of this hymn, in which the text of Psalm 124 has been greatly expanded.

38  The text of the farce is preceded by the following "Argument" (synopsis): "Gros Guillaume goes on a business trip, entrusts his daughter to Turlupin. Sir Horace comes to have her in marriage. Turlupin tries to kill him, then he recognizes him and asks for tokens to bring to his beloved Florentine. Sir Horace gives him a chain, and he [Turlupin] keeps it. The marriage is performed, the father comes back from the business trip, then they all beat one another."

39  The widow Ducarroy specialized in the publication of topical and satirical works. Curiously, she had issued in 1617 a poem entitled "Brief Account of the Life, Death, and Funeral of the Marquis d'Ancre."

40  This page was probably not written by the author of the play. It is doubtful that the playwright would have rehashed the standard comments about fortune, unless it was meant tongue in cheek. As for the plot synopsis, the Argument calls Mordecai the queen's uncle, as in the Vulgate, whereas in the play he refers to himself as her cousin (v. 337), as in the Hebrew text. The mention of a two-day interval between Mordecai's special honor and the downfall of Haman corresponds neither to the Biblical account nor to the play. The awkward syntax suggests that the passage was hastily composed.

41  Acheron is one of the rivers in Hades. Characters in mythology usually preferred to swear by another of its rivers, the Styx (cf. v. 535).

42  This boasting speech is reminiscent of passages in tragedies of the late sixteenth century, including the opening soliloquy in Montchrestien's *Haman*. Although humorously presented here, the idea that human warriors can successfully fight against (pagan) gods goes back as far as

Homer.
43 In the Bible Ahasuerus gives the banquet during the third year of his reign.
44 The choice of instruments suggests a concert of Renaissance, rather than ancient, music. The same remark applies to the menu, as elaborated in the next speech.
45 This passage seems to imply that Vashti's banishment and Esther's coronation are not yet definitive.
46 The description of Esther's beauty is in the style of Renaissance love poetry; it might have been inspired by the king's speech in the 1601 version of *Haman* (see the introduction to that play).
47 Duranda's speech is puzzling, and at times the literal meaning is hard to determine. Why a devil should be the victim, rather than the torturer, is never explained. The conflation (frequent in Renaissance texts) of the pagan Hades, ruled by Pluto, and the Christian hell, filled with cauldrons and instruments of torture, does not simplify matters. At the end of the soliloquy Duranda suddenly identifies with the role of the tempter, which medieval drama often assigned to devils, even though by destroying Haman he stands to lose the life of ease and good food that first brought him to the minister's house.
48 This expression is apparently based on the Latin saying "Asini caput ne laves nitro" (Don't wash an ass's head with lye), which Erasmus glossed as "Don't expend much money or labor on a vile and filthy matter" (*Adages* III.3.39). A sixteenth-century collection of proverbs gives a slightly different version: "A laver la tête d'un âne / L'on n'y perd que la lessive" (By washing an ass's head one wastes only the lye). Rabelais also refers to this proverb (V.21).
49 The sense is unclear. Perhaps this is a reference to a medieval French proverb, "En peau de brebis ce que tu voudras écris" (Write whatever you like in a sheep's skin).
50 The original puns on "planetes" and "plats nets."
51 The reference is to the fate of Sisyphus, who was punished for disobedience to the gods. We never learn what, if anything, Duranda is punished for.
52 Orcus is one of the Latin names for the underworld.
53 At this point Duranda addresses the audience and treats them as his accomplices (cf. v. 342).
54 This line is a parody of Nebuchadnezzar's boasting speech in Garnier's *Les Juives*, one of the best-known tragedies of the sixteenth century. The striking similarities between Haman's soliloquy and the king's speech in Act I make Haman look all the more foolish.
55 The contradiction between "in the next few days" and "within this hour" contributes to the comic effect.

56 Mordecai's insistence on Haman's plebeian origin is not derived from the Bible, where Haman is said to have descended from Agag, the generic name for Amalekite kings, or from the Apocrypha, which describes him as a Macedonian (16.10).
57 Mordecai makes no reference to the danger threatening his people and thinks only of saving his own life.
58 Except for brief mentions of the king (v. 346) and the banquet (v. 351), there is no direct link between this farcical episode and the rest of the play.
59 The French is unclear.
60 The French text spells the names Agathan and Thirsan; the Vulgate has Bagathan and Thares. In order not to confuse the reader, I have used the standard English spellings.
61 The suggestion that the eunuchs planned to assassinate the nobles, as well as the king, was added by the playwright.
62 Although not indicated in the original, there is clearly a change of speaker at vv. 463, 545, 553.
63 The playwright neglects to give Haman an aside, alerting the audience that he expects himself to be the recipient of the honor he is proposing.
64 Time is speeded up, since Haman must parade Mordecai all through the streets of the capital and be back in the palace only 47 lines later.
65 In the Bible there is an interval of eleven months between the promulgation of the edict and the date scheduled for it to be carried out.
66 This suggests that Haman used the royal seal without the king's permission. If so, there is a parallel with Duranda's unauthorized use of Pluto's seal.
67 This anachronism adds to the comic effect.
68 In the Bible the gallows was raised a more impressive fifty cubits high (roughly 75 feet).
69 H. C. Lancaster notes the similarities between this line and a line from the anonymous play *La Magicienne étrangère* (1617) that had openly attacked Leonora Galligai, the wife of Concini: "Allons, c'est trop longtemps en ce lieu caqueté" (Come on, you have babbled too long in this place). There is no way to prove whether this is or is not a coincidence.

Printed in Canada